*Dedicated to all
my beloved students*

KIDS SPEAK

Children Talk
About Themselves

by Chaim Walder

translated by Shifra Slater

Illustrated by Yoni Gerstein

FELDHEIM
Jerusalem □ New York

Originally published in 1993 in Hebrew
as *Yeladim Mesaprim al Atzmam*

First published 1994
ISBN 0-87306-672-3

FELDHEIM PUBLISHERS
POB 35002 / Jerusalem, Israel

200 Airport Executive Park
Nanuet, NY 10954

www.feldheim.com

typeset at Astronel, Jerusalem

Printed in Israel

A Note to Parents

Encouraging children to talk about themselves is the key to helping them overcome their problems and fears. As a teacher of young children, I have discovered that while this may take time and great patience on our part, children do want to confide their worries and to be helped by their parents and teachers.

Although most of my other works deal with adults, I have always found myself drawn to writing about children. I believe that every writer dreams of writing about a world which is somehow better and truer than the one we live in. I have found that sought-after, enchanted place in the world of children. It is a world of pure values, of dignity and truth.

Writing for children and about them is a labor of love, which aims to reach out and touch, but not to tamper or interfere.

— C.W.

6

Acknowledgments

I would like to thank those who gave me the confidence and opportunity to express myself through my pen: the editorial staff of the newspaper *Yated Ne'eman*. Their support and encouragement, and their helpful advice, have proved invaluable to me.

I must also pay tribute to the renowned educator, Rabbi Meir Munk, *shlita*, director of Talmud Torah Toras Emes, who was kind enough to go through the manuscript and to add or delete where he found it necessary to do so. The educational insights which he skillfully wove into the stories enhanced the purpose of this book: to help children to express their thoughts and emotions and thereby deal with their problems.

I am grateful to Feldheim Publishers and its editorial and graphic departments for their work in preparing the English edition for publication.

I would like to extend my gratitude and appreciation to Shifra Slater for her careful English translation.

I thank my dear parents, whose character, love, and devotion to education account for all the good which is in me.

Praised above all women is my wife, and blessed also are my dear sons, Meir Zvi and Moshe. In them lie the roots of my success up to this point, and the reasons why, God willing, I shall continue on this path.

Chaim Walder
Bnei Brak
Kislev 5754

מכתבו של המחנך הדגול הרה"ג ר' מאיר מונק שליט"א

מנהל חינוכי בת"ת "תורת אמת" ב"ב

בס"ד מוצש"ק פר' וארא תשנ"ג

לידידי הרב חיים ולדר שליט"א

ר.ב. בזה החומר הסיפורי שכתבת.

לבקשתך עברתי עליו והערתי הערות בקורתיות, מלבד ההערות נראה
החומר חינוכי ונחוץ, כי הוא נוגע בבעיות יום יומיות מחיי הילדים בבית
ובחברה, ומציע להם פתרונות מעשיים שיוכלו להשתלט על הבעיה בכוחות
עצמם.

מה טוב לו הי' מתרבה חומר קריאה מסוג זה.

בידידות
מאיר מונק

Approbation from **Rabbi Meir Munk**, *shlita*

RABBI YITZCHAK SILBERSTEIN Rabbi of Ramat Elchanan **BNEI-BRAK**	יצחק זילברשטיין רב שכונת רמת אלחנן בני-ברק

בס"ד, יום _____

[handwritten Hebrew letter — text illegible for accurate transcription]

Approbation from Rabbi Yitzchak Silberstein, *shlita*

בס"ד, בני-ברק, יום א' ל... ואלה השמות

אולי שלום לסופרים...

להרב חיים ולבי שיחי'

ראיתי את ספרין היקר ולהתינוק והיתי לי לב של קרית רוח ולשמחה

ואכן ראויים הדברים אלו לומדם

לה... נוקר בצמרתינו התינוקת היא הקרית הרול... חשובה נוגעים

... ובכים בהתנהאות ... בין תלמיד ...

ואמ...ת כאן העניר את נפש הילד ומהעשאו אדרבם

... ולדו יכו ... רבבו כתב את

קהילת לב... ופתחו... באתר ... היום יום ש

הבין ... לתהיר...

ובזה אסיי ל... ה ... יברך ... ורבי. הסטי וסיק את הקהלות

הנכבסת ... והיא ... לדעת תלמירים ... הגאון הכולית

בא...ת שלום ... לקם מקונין התורה הקדוש ה

בתקי...

אברהם גומבו שלישו

Approbation from **Rabbi Avraham Gombo**, *shlita*

To My Young Readers

There are many, many children in the world — and each and every one *is* an entire world.

Everybody has moments of joy and moments of sadness, of tears and of laughter. Each of you can think of things that frighten you or make you worry, and things that make you feel good inside.

And yet, even though your own life is different from any other child's, there *are* things which you all have in common. And if you realize that, you can learn how to deal with problems which you might have thought only you have.

In this book, I have collected the stories of thirty-four children. Every one of you should be able to see yourself — or a feeling or situation similar to your own — somewhere among the stories these children tell about themselves.

As a teacher of children around your age, I know that a problem can find its solution only if you are able to talk about it. Because if you keep it a secret, the problem will remain inside your heart and might grow so big that you can't bear it.

Most of the time, your mother or father, your teacher, or even a friend, will be able to help you solve your problem. But first, you must tell them what's troubling you.

If any of you would like to write to me, I will be happy to receive your letters. You can write to: KIDS SPEAK, P.O.B. 211, Bnei Brak, Israel. With Hashem's help, I will answer you.

Happy reading!

Chaim Walder

Contents

Shorty

My name is Ze'ev. I'm in fifth grade. I'm not really special in any way — not in schoolwork or in sports, and not socially either. If anything, I'm the laziest kid in the class. But there is one thing about me that makes me stand out. I'm really, really short — short and skinny. I look like I'm in second grade, not fifth.

Every time I look in the mirror, I ask Hashem when I'm going to grow. It's really hard to have to look up at my friends all the time, and to hear people on the crowded bus every morning say, "Keep moving, Shorty."

My friends treat me like a nothing. They know I'm lazy and that I don't know even the stuff they learned in third grade — well, almost.

So my life is pretty gloomy, but I never really thought it'd be different. I've always been short and lazy, and I thought I'd always be like that. That's how I figured it. So I never laughed much, and I never felt good about myself. I just felt small.

The truth is that there is one thing I'm good at, not that it's anything very important. I'm the class "Information Bureau." I know everything that's going on. How? Well, first of all, I read a lot. But besides that, I have ways of finding out all kinds of things, inside school and out. Somehow, I'm the one who knows when this year's school trip will be, who's going to be our teacher next year, what they've been talking about in the teachers' lounge, and how much sugar the eighth-grade teacher takes in his coffee.

In these things, I'm the expert. Whenever a kid needs some information, I'm the one he'll turn to. It's my only chance to talk and to feel like maybe I'm worth something. (Even though I really know that these things are dumb, and nobody respects me very much for knowing them.)

In the middle of the year, our class got a new teacher, Rabbi Samuels. Naturally, I was able to tell everyone where he lives, the school he had taught in before, where he was born, and which of his relatives I happened to know! Of course, the main thing they all wanted to know was whether he was nice or strict. I told them that that remained to be seen.

As soon as he came into our classroom, we

saw that Rabbi Samuels was both things: nice *and* strict. The look in his eye said very clearly that he would not stand for any nonsense or disturbance. At the same time, he smiled at us a lot and we could see he was really a nice person.

Well, it didn't take him very long to discover who was the lazy one in the class. Right away, he started taking a firm hand with me. He insisted that I do all my homework, and do it right. He'd even call my house the night before a test to ask my parents if I was studying! All in all, he didn't ever let me take it easy! Where all the teachers before him had given up on me pretty quickly, and taken an attitude of "Whatever you want, kid — it's up to you," this Rabbi Samuels kept giving me a hard time. Actually I saw that, for some reason, he really cared what would become of me.

One day, in the middle of the morning, he asked me to come with him to the teachers' lounge. When I saw a substitute walk in to take over the class, I knew I was in for a long lecture!

Rabbi Samuels started by asking me all kinds of questions. I could tell he understood me. He asked me to tell him about my good points and my bad points, and I answered him. I spoke about a lot of things that troubled me, and even told him things that I had always kept to myself. But I left out one thing. After I finished talking, he said, "You forgot something, didn't you?" I didn't answer. I couldn't even nod my head.

"Okay," he said. "I see that it's difficult for you to tell me, so I'll tell you. You're short. It bothers you. It hurts you. It makes you feel... kind of worthless. Right?"

For some reason, I burst into tears. Tears from inside my heart, where all the hurt had been hiding, and which my teacher had uncovered with his words. I cried and cried, and I wasn't even embarrassed. And he let me cry and didn't say a word.

Later, when I calmed down, Rabbi Samuels took a picture out of his pocket. It was a photograph of a little kid around eight years old, in a jacket and hat, dressed up like a little man. The boy was facing a crowd of people and gesturing with his hand, as though he was making a speech.

"See that little boy?" asked the teacher. "How old does he look to you?"

I answered: "About eight years old, I'd say."

The teacher smiled and said, "That's a bar-mitzvah boy, Ze'ev. He's *thirteen* and he's giving his *derashah* here."

I took the picture back from him and looked at it more carefully. The boy looked even smaller than me, and I'm eleven! Then I looked at the teacher's face, and looked back at the picture, and I understood....

He smiled — almost laughed — and said, "Yes, that's me. I was even shorter than you. But I never felt so bad about it. I knew I had a talent for speaking well, and so I never thought I was any worse off than the other kids. And as for them, when they saw that I had confidence in myself, they treated me accordingly, and never paid any attention to my height. Meanwhile," my teacher added, "I was using the gifts that Hashem did give me. Any time there was a class party or special event, I got up and spoke. And I wasn't shy. Here, look at this picture. See what a shorty I was at my bar mitzvah, and there I am making a speech just like a grown-up! And, you know what — I think everyone enjoyed my speech too.

"A while later, in high school, I started to grow. Today, even though I'm certainly not a tall man, there's nothing so unusual about my height."

His story was finished, but he added, "Ze'evi, I understood what your problem was from the very first day. I hope you'll take a lesson from my story, and stop ruining your life for a silly reason."

Rabbi Samuels handed me a tissue to dry

my eyes. He looked at his watch. Two hours had passed from the time we left the classroom, and neither of us had noticed.

Well, you might not believe it, but it's seven months later now, and I'm a different kid! All the schoolwork that I was missing because of my laziness, I've managed to make up, with help from my parents and from Rabbi Samuels. I did it surprisingly quickly, too, and now I'm even among the better students in the class. I stopped being so sensitive about my height, and I now realize that if *I* don't pay attention to it, no one *else* does either. They probably never even cared about how short I was at all!

If any of you is short like me, take my advice: Don't be ashamed of it. Even if you're really, really short, there's nothing to be ashamed of. A person's real height is spiritual, not physical. He can reach true heights in good *middos*, in *yiras Shamayim*, and in his Torah learning. Nothing else matters.

The Boy Who Started the Fire

My name is Yoni. I live in Haifa, and I'm in fourth grade.

My house is on a quiet side street. In fact, lots of people had never heard of our street, because nothing unusual ever happened on it. Until last year.

Then, one evening, sirens filled the air and within minutes, the street was full of fire trucks, ambulances, and police cars.

Like all the children in the neighborhood, I ran after the gigantic red trucks, and pretty soon I saw why they were there.

The building at number 30 was on fire! Through the windows, you could see the flames. It was very scary. The firemen set up a ladder so the people inside the apartments could climb down. Some of them had little children in their arms.

As soon as they had gotten everyone out, the firemen were able to put out the fire. Meanwhile, the police began to question people to find out how it started.

I was standing with a bunch of kids, when suddenly Nechemia, who lives in my building, ran up. "I bet I know who started this fire," he said excitedly.

"Who?" we all asked together.

"Nisanowitz's son," said Nechemia. "I saw a policeman point to him and say, '*That's him,*' to another policeman."

We ran over to the ambulance, and, sure enough, Nisanowitz's son, a boy of about fourteen, was sitting inside.

Well, the fire was finally out. Everything was black and smokey. There was a whole lot of damage. Nisanowitz's apartment was completely burned, and some of the neighbors' apartments too.

The tenants were all put up in hotels. It took a month to fix up all the apartments. Then they all returned home.

One day after school, we were playing in the park. Suddenly, Srulik began to chant, "There — goes — the — boy — that — set — the — fire — oy, oy —" All heads turned to see Nisanowitz's son. He turned red and walked away quickly. Actually, he's more a teenager than a *boy*, but with us kids, anyone who isn't a man yet is still called a boy.

From that day on, every time we saw him, we'd all shout, "There goes the boy — that set the fire — oy, oy!" At first, he would just walk away from us, but after we'd yelled those words at him a few times, he started to chase us.

We always ran off fast in different directions, and he never managed to catch us.

Now that I look back, I can't imagine how we could have been so mean. I guess kids just don't think about what they're doing, and don't think about how another person feels.

A few months went by like that, and Nisanowitz's son started looking sad and got kind of quiet. But we didn't pay any attention to that. For us, it was fun to keep calling out our usual line, and waiting for him to try to catch us.

One day we were playing as usual, when the bus stopped and out came... Nisanowitz's son. As always, we lined up and started singing, "There goes the boy —"

But this time, the kid looked really mad, and started after us. His face was twisted with anger. Everyone ran fast, including me, but I tripped over Moshe's bike, and fell flat on the ground.

My knees and elbows really hurt, but I hardly felt it because of how scared I was of Nisanowitz's son. He stood right over me, and I started screaming. He pulled me to my feet and I knew he was going to give me a bad beating. I started crying and screaming, even though I knew it wouldn't help.

But instead of hitting me, he asked in a calm voice: "Are you hurt? I'm sorry that you fell because of me."

I was shocked. What was going on? Instead of a beating, I got an apology! I stopped crying, and stared at him in amazement.

"Sit down a minute," he told me. I sat down on a bench, and he sat down beside me.

"How do you feel?" he asked.

"I'm okay," I mumbled.

"I've been wanting to ask you something," he said. "Maybe you can give me the answer. Why do you kids think I started the fire?" I hesitated, and he said, "Go ahead, tell me; you see you don't have to be afraid of me."

Quietly, I answered. "The day of the fire, a boy said he heard a policeman say that *you* were the one who started the fire, and we really did see you in the ambulance...."

The bigger boy looked shocked. "What? That's what the policeman said? Listen, I'll tell you what really happened."

And this is the story he told me: "That night I was alone in the house with my little sister. I turned on the light in her room, and all of a sudden I heard a small explosion — and a flame shot out of the lamp. Then the curtains next to it caught fire. I was too shocked to move, but I got hold of myself, and tried to think what to do. I ran into the kitchen and filled a pot with water. I threw the water at the fire, but it continued to spread, and the flames started getting close to the bed where my little sister was sleeping.

"My parents weren't home, like I said," the boy went on, "and I knew that it was my responsibility to save my little sister. In the meantime, the flames were spreading all over the room, and the smoke was beginning to choke me.

"I woke my sister up, and said: 'Come on, quick! There's a fire and we have to get out of here.' She was scared, and started screaming. The smoke was making it very hard for us to breathe. 'Come on!' I yelled, but she was hysterical, and wouldn't budge. By this time, the door had started to burn, and I knew we didn't have much time left. I grabbed my sister in both arms, and ran out of the bedroom. The hallway was full of smoke and I almost couldn't see the way to the front door.

"Suddenly, I tripped on something and fell down. My hand was thrown forward, and it hit

something that was on fire, and got burned. Then I couldn't hear my sister screaming anymore, and I was afraid that something terrible had happened to her. The smoke was so thick I couldn't see her. With tremendous effort, I got myself up, and pulled myself toward the door. It was starting to burn too. The heat was unbearable! I managed to open the door and to get out into the hall. Then the pain and the smoke were too much and I fainted.

"When I woke up, I found myself in the ambulance. The policemen were all praising me for being so brave. They said I had saved my sister's life. What a relief to hear that my sister was alive! At that point I felt that the pain and the injury were all worthwhile.

"Well, after we came back from the hotel to our repaired home, my world fell apart. I don't know why, but suddenly the children were calling me 'the boy who started the fire.' At first I didn't pay any attention, but then *all* the kids in the neighborhood started saying it. Sometimes, when I'm just walking by a house, I'll hear children call out the window, 'There's the boy who started the fire.' It's embarrassing. It really hurts. Why do you do it, why do you say that?" asked the boy, with tears glistening in his eyes.

I looked around and I saw that all the kids

who had been playing with me were standing behind our bench, not saying a word. I guess they had seen that he was talking to me, and that he wasn't doing me any harm, so they came up close and heard the story.

Now Nechemia did something really brave. He tapped Nisanowitz's son on the shoulder and said, "Listen, it's all my fault. I'm the one who saw the policeman say, 'That's him.' I was sure that he meant you were the one who had started the fire! But now I see what a terrible mistake I made. I beg you, with all my heart, to forgive me."

The teenager looked at him for a moment, and then said, "I forgive you, but on one condition. From now on, you must learn to always check into things, and not jump to conclusions. You must learn to be *dan l'chaf zechus*, to judge others favorably, and you must never speak *lashon ha-ra* to others. Also, you should try not to hurt people. You don't know how much pain you caused me." Then he got up and said, "Be seeing you, kids," and he turned and walked slowly off to his house.

We stayed in the park, silent and ashamed. "I think," I began, breaking the silence, "that we have to do something for him, to make up somehow for the terrible thing we've done."

"Let's buy him a present," Moshe suggested.

So each one of us chipped in, and the next day we went and bought a silver *kiddush* cup. We stood and waited at the entrance to building number 30. When the boy finally came home, we handed him the package. He looked at us, unwrapped it, and stared at the gleaming cup as if he just couldn't believe his eyes. Then he looked at the base of the cup, where we had engraved: *For the hero who saved his sister from the fire.* Tears sprang to his eyes.

That's the story, kids. I don't think I have to tell you what the lesson is. I, for one, really learned a lot from what happened. I sure hope I'll never again suspect people who are innocent! And never ever hurt somebody's feelings the way we did, or embarrass anyone in public like that.

A Happy Birthday???

My name is Chava. I'm in third grade.

I'm a regular girl, like anybody else. I don't have any special problems at all. But something happened in my class that I want to tell you about. And... well, why make such a long introduction? Let me just start!

Last week, Shulamis — the daughter of the shul's *shammes* — announced that she was having a birthday party in her house, on Monday at seven o'clock. All the girls, including me, were really happy, and everyone said they'd be thrilled to come.

But then, on Sunday, Shira also made an announcement. Her birthday party would *also* be on Monday, in *her* house, at *seven o'clock*!

Well, Shira's father is very rich. They live in a big, fancy house, and every year she makes an unforgettable birthday party! There are delicious cakes, every kind of candy you can imagine, exciting games, and *big* prizes for everybody.

Shulamis asked Shira if she could make her party on a different day, since *she* had announced *hers* first, and everything was already prepared.

But Shira was not interested. "You move *your* party," she told Shulamis, and refused to even think about changing her own plans.

Monday came. The girls in the class didn't talk about which party they were going to, but everyone knew that nobody would be willing to miss Shira's terrific party.

At six o'clock on Monday, I still didn't know which girl's party I would go to. On the one hand, I knew that if I went to Shulamis' I'd be missing out on a lot of good games and candy and great prizes. On the other hand, I felt really sorry for Shulamis, thinking of how she'd feel when nobody came. My heart just ached for her.

At a quarter to seven, I was still trying to decide.

At ten to seven, I left my house, and my feet seemed to have a mind of their own. All of a sudden, there I was, at the door of... Shulamis' house.

I knocked, and when she opened the door, I saw an empty living room — empty of kids, that is. There were lots of chairs and balloons. No one had come. Shulamis smiled bravely at me. Her mother said, "I guess they're all a little late."

I nodded, but I felt really awful. At seven-fifteen, Shulamis stopped smiling. She just kept looking at her watch, at the door, and back again....

Finally, she asked me, "Do you think *all* the other girls went to Shira's party?"

I shrugged. "I dunno."

With every minute that passed, Shulamis' face fell lower. Then I saw a tear in the corner of her eye, and then another, and another.

She went into the other room, and I heard her sobbing quietly.

I made a decision.

I went into the kitchen and asked Shulamis' mother if I could use the phone. I found Shira's number and, nervously, I called her house.

A woman answered. In the background, I could hear laughing voices.

"H...h...hello," I stammered. "This is Chava, Shira's friend."

"Hello, Chava! Why haven't you come to the party?" asked Shira's mother.

I hesitated but then I screwed up my courage, and I said, "While all those girls are laughing in your house, there's one girl who's crying."

I couldn't believe I had said it.

Shira's mother was surprised too. "Which

girl is crying?" she asked.

"Shulamis," I answered, and I told her the whole story.

Shira's mother listened to me quietly. She sighed, and said, "Chava, I really appreciate your calling to tell me this. Please tell Shulamis that a surprise is on the way."

Well, sure enough, less than ten minutes later, there was a loud knocking on the door. Shulamis ran to open it. Can you guess who was standing at the door, holding a big platter with a gorgeous cake on it? Shira!

Behind her stood all the rest of the girls in the class. They all came in, and sat down on the chairs which Shulamis' mother had set up.

One of the girls whispered the story to me. Shira's mother had stopped the party immediately and said, "This is a terrible thing. This is no birthday party! It's shaming another person. It's like murder!"

Shira had turned really red. Her mother said to her, "I want *you* to decide what you have to do now. One thing is for sure: I am stopping this birthday party immediately."

Shira thought for a minute, and said, "Okay, let's go. Let's take all these cakes, candy, games, and prizes over to Shulamis."

"So here we are," she finished.

Well, that party turned out to be the happiest

one I ever saw. All the girls sang so loudly, and they put Shira and Shulamis at the head of the table. They were smiling at each other all the time, just smiling with shining faces.

When the party was over, everyone wished Shira and Shulamis "*mazal tov*," got two bags stuffed with goodies — one from Shira and one from Shulamis — and went home. I was the only one left.

"Well, what do you say to the surprise they all made you?" I asked Shulamis. But she didn't answer. She just came over to me, held my hand tightly in hers, and looked into my eyes. Then she said, "Chava, I know what happened. I think the best part of the surprise is finding out what a wonderful friend I have in the class." The look in her eyes told me that she really did know the whole story. I just smiled.

"Thank you," Shulamis added simply. And the happiness that I felt right then was not like any other happiness I ever felt in my whole life.

Responsibility

My name is Uri. I'm in third grade. I live in Yerushalayim.

It may be hard for you to believe my story, but it's true. I'm eight years old, and I'm the oldest kid in our family. I have a sister who's five and a brother who's four, and I'm in charge of them. I don't just watch them, I mean I really take care of them: I listen to what they have to say, and I...well, I teach them things.

At home, I do all the important things. If the phone rings, I'm the one who answers. And if someone comes from the electric company, or if anyone at all comes, I'm the one who lets him in and tells him what to do.

When my father has something to do in the city, he takes me along with him so that I can take care of it.

You probably think that I'm putting you on, but I can explain it all in one sentence: My father and my mother are deaf-mutes.

They don't hear a thing and they cannot speak. They can read lips, and actually, my father is able to make sounds with his mouth — but he doesn't talk like other people, so no one understands him except me.

Don't get me wrong. Nobody has to feel sorry for us or anything. My father and my mother both go to work, and we get along just fine. My mother's a great cook. We're a very happy family. But, believe me, it's not easy being responsible for so much at my age, and sometimes I feel like there's a heavy weight on my shoulders.

Like that first night when the missiles from Iraq landed — I was the one who heard the siren. I woke my parents, and explained to them (in sign language) that there was an alarm. Then I had to calm my brother and sister down. They were really scared. I was too, but I tried not to let them see.

During all the nights of the war, I hardly slept at all. At the end of the war, I agreed to take turns with my brother and sister (both of them are also able to hear and to speak).

There was a time when it used to be easier for me, when my grandmother was still healthy. It's thanks to her, in fact, that I learned how to speak normally — and I'm the best reader in my class! But now my grandmother is sick and she can't help me the way she used to.

There are all kinds of funny things I could tell you. Like when there's a parent-teacher's meeting, I come along and explain to my father — with my hands — what kind of kid I am. Lucky thing I'm a good student, or else...

At the year-end assembly last year, the principal said: "I would like to present a very special boy to you. He is someone from whom you can all learn the meaning of honoring parents and what real responsibility is."

To my surprise, I heard him call my name. Then it was impossible to hear anything because of the loud applause. And, for some reason, I saw that my parents were crying. Really crying.

Anyway, I would like to ask of you kids just one thing: If you should meet my father somewhere, don't laugh at the strange noises that he makes. It's not his fault! He is a good father — just look at the family he managed to raise.

I'm really proud of him!

Writing Right and Righting Wrongs

My name is Avigail. I'm in fifth grade. I could be one of the best students, but I have a problem. A double problem: my spelling and my handwriting.

The mistakes I make in spelling are horrendous, and my handwriting is even worse.

In fact, if my mother hadn't helped me write this out, believe me, you wouldn't understand a word. Want to see? This is the way I started the story, before showing it to my mother: *Mi nam iz Havigail, im en fith grad.*

You may think it's funny, but that is exactly how my sentences come out. What's more, my handwriting is so messy that I myself can't figure out what letters I meant to write.

All my teachers started out telling me gently

to try and improve my handwriting and to study correct spelling. So I tried, but it didn't seem that anything improved.

When the teachers saw that gentle remarks were not doing the trick, they switched to a stricter line. One teacher simply ignored any work that was written poorly (and that was *all* of it). She explained that she could not toler- ate such terrible mistakes, because it would encourage me to continue to write like that.

"Look," she said, "an occasional mistake like *terible* or *beleve* would be one thing, but when you write *en* instead of *in* and leave out all your silent e's, you show me that you simply don't know how to write the language. And I will not mark homework that is written in another language."

One of my teachers handled my spelling problem another way. She would write one of my sentences on the board, like *The jus wondrd furti yirs in the dezert.* Then she wrote, TRANSLATION: *The Jews wandered forty years in the desert.* Everyone in the class had a good laugh, but I wanted to cry. Why did she have to embarrass me like that? I wondered. Why would she want to humiliate me? I'm sure she really wanted to force me to do something about it, but it had the opposite effect. I just stopped writing altogether, because I was afraid they'd make fun of me.

Well, this year we got a new teacher. Hesitantly, I handed him my answers to his first homework assignment. He threw me a look right away, and said jokingly, "Hey! I see you write with *mistooks!*" He said it without anger, and without scorn, and we both laughed.

After that, he took my notebooks and studied them for a long time. I saw how hard he had to work in order to decipher my hieroglyphics and to figure out which words I meant. At last, he wrote my grade: "Contents: EXCELLENT. Spelling and penmanship: FAR LESS."

I wasn't offended. I knew that the mark was exactly right. I saw that he appreciated the knowledge that I had, but that he objected to the way it was written.

After a few days of giving me marks like that, the new teacher finally said to me — without anger, and without making a "big deal" out of it — "Listen, Avigail, we have to do something about your spelling mistakes."

Then he told me, "When I was a kid, my handwriting was awful too, but I managed to change it in an unusual way. I bought myself a special notebook, and on each page I would write one letter very carefully. Then I wrote it over and over again, until I got used to writing legible, neat letters, inside the lines. Next, I bought another notebook and started practicing whole words so that I could learn to avoid spelling mistakes. Within half a year, believe it or not, my handwriting had improved tremendously, and my terrible spelling mistakes had just about disappeared."

When the teacher had finished telling me his story he added, "Look, Avigail, I'm not telling *you* what to do. You can think about it, and decide for yourself."

That day, he took my notebook, and gave me the following mark: "Contents: EXCELLENT. Spelling and penmanship: COULD CHANGE, *IF*..." I understood.

That very day, I bought a brand new notebook and started to write the letters, one at a time, concentrating real hard. Slowly but surely, I got through the entire alphabet. I bought a second notebook, and I went through the whole thing all over again. Believe it or not, my handwriting now looks nothing at all like the handwriting I had before.

This week, I bought another new notebook, and I'm starting to practice writing whole words. I really think there's a chance those awful spelling mistakes of mine will completely disappear, once and for all. And it's all because of my teacher. I'll be grateful to him forever.

I'm sure there must be other kids out there with a problem like mine. I recommend to all of you that you try this method. It really works. You'll see results immediately.

Now I realize how much I was missing all those years. What a shame. But — better late than never.

The Wheelchair Athlete

I saw him for the first time when we were in the baseball field, playing softball. There he was, sitting at the edge of the field. He wasn't playing, but his eyes followed that ball, and you could see he really wanted to grab hold of it.

You could read everything on his pale face. You could see the joy when someone caught the ball and scored. And you could see how bad he felt when one of the boys was out.

Sometimes, the ball would roll into the street, and then his pleasant face would reveal sudden tension and concern, and his eyes would dart in both directions to see if any cars were coming.

No, we didn't invite him to join our game. We knew he couldn't leave his wheelchair.

His face was unfamiliar to me. Apparently,

his family had moved into the neighborhood only two weeks earlier. I didn't know his name or the name of his family, but I was especially curious to know why he was in that wheelchair, unable to run and play like the rest of us.

Once in a while, the ball would practically roll right into his hands. He would throw it back to us quickly, his face shining with joy and satisfaction.

I asked the other kids to throw the ball in his direction every few minutes, as if by accident, just so I could see that look of happiness on his face.

From time to time, he would circle the playing field in his wheelchair at top speed, as though to prove to himself that he could also move fast.

During one of his trips around the field, his wheelchair suddenly twisted and turned over. The boy fell out of it, right onto the ground. We all ran over and gently lifted him back into the chair. He didn't cry, even though his face gave away the pain he was feeling. He whispered a "thank you" and then continued his silence.

I decided to leave the game and sit down beside him. "Do you want me to take you home?" I asked. He answered, "Oh, no. I love watching you play."

After a while, I finally found the courage and asked: "What's your name?"

"Yitzchak," he said. "And yours?"

"Meir," I said. And we both fell silent.

The next day, his mother brought him back to the field to watch us play. His hands were bandaged, a reminder of the previous day's fall.

I told the kids to play without me. "I want to sit with him for a while," I explained. I sat next to him, but I couldn't think of anything to talk to him about.

"Could I take you home after the game?" I asked.

"Sure, no problem," he said, and smiled.

I went back to playing with the other guys, and we kept up our routine of throwing the ball in Yitzchak's direction. He was getting good at it, and by now he would throw the ball back with a practiced hand, calling out gleefully and laughing. We all had a great time.

After the game, I wheeled him to his house.

He lived on the ground floor. At his request, I knocked at the door. His mother looked at him, her eyes round with surprise. "Why didn't you wait for me to bring you home?" she asked softly. Then she turned to me. "And who are you?" I hesitated, looking at Yitzchak and then back at his mother.

"He's my friend," Yitzchak answered for me. "I know him from the baseball field. He's the one I told you about — the guy who gets the kids to

pretend they're losing the ball, to make me feel like I'm part of the game."

I turned red as a beet. I hadn't realized he knew what we were doing....

They invited me inside. His room was decorated with great big, beautiful, pictures on all the walls. In the corner of every picture was a small signature: *Yitzchak*. I gazed at them all without saying a word.

"You have a really nice room," I said finally. "And your drawings are just amazing."

"Thanks," he said simply. "I like to draw. Now, tell me about yourself."

I started telling him about myself. I told him I was in fifth grade, that I was a pretty good student, but sometimes a little wild. I told him about our class. I told him about the teachers and about my friends and all of a sudden I found myself pouring out some of the deepest feelings in my heart to him. It felt good.

When I stopped, Yitzchak said, "I see that you're embarrassed to ask me what I'm doing in this wheelchair. So I'll tell you myself.

"I was a regular kid, just like you," he began. "I was the fastest and the best ball player in the class. I played like you and I was almost always the winner.

"One time, the ball started rolling, and it ended up in the middle of the street. I ran after it, and then..." His voice began to tremble. "Then a car came out of nowhere and hit me. I went flying, and it was just lucky that I landed on my legs and not on my head. If I'd landed on my head, I wouldn't be sitting here now. But even this way, it's no picnic, believe me. I can't move my legs at all. That's why I'm stuck in this wheelchair. I hope that someday I'll get better, but it's going to take a long time and a lot of hard work. I thank Hashem every day that He saved my life, and that my hands weren't injured. I can still do just about anything I want with them."

Now I understood why Yitzchak was stricken with such fear every time the ball rolled into the street.

We kept on talking, and I realized that he was a lot smarter than me. In Gemara and Chumash he knew the answers to any questions I asked him, but he had questions for me that I couldn't answer. He told me lots of interesting things about satellites and space ships that go to the moon, and about faraway countries. And he told everything in such an entertaining and amusing way that it was really fun to sit and listen to him.

Suddenly, we looked out the window and saw that it was getting dark. We both said at the same time, "Wow, look how time flies!" We laughed. We just hadn't felt the hours passing. I rushed to phone my mother, who had already started to worry about me. I reassured her, and said goodbye to my new friend.

Now, Yitzchak goes to our school, and all the kids in the class like him. But if you ever see a boy pushing a wheelchair with a cute, skinny kid in it, you can assume it's me and Yitzchak. He's my very best friend. I'm so glad that I met him, and I'll never ever leave him.

Sometimes now, the rest of us guys help him out of his wheelchair and he manages to walk a few steps. Yitzchak told us that his doctor and physiotherapist told his mother that he's made a lot of progress lately! Soon, with Hashem's help, he'll be walking and running like the rest of us.

Meanwhile, we're all enjoying his talented hands. The walls of our classroom are covered with great big beautiful murals and drawings. At the bottom of each, in small letters, it says "*Yitzchak.*"

Power

My name is Yochai. I'm really strong. In fact, I'm strong enough to pick up any two kids in my class at once.

But I never use my strength to do bad things or to bully anyone. If someone starts up with me, I never use my fists. I just try to calm things down.

Once somebody said to me: "Yochai, how come you never want to fight? I think you're chicken." I just kept quiet. I don't care if that's what he thinks. I don't think fighting shows you're brave — I think it shows that you're stupid.

I have a good friend in my class, a boy named Benny.

Benny's a short, skinny kid, and when we walk around together, people think I'm his big brother.

Size is not the only way we're different from

each other. He's quiet — he almost never talks, and I talk all the time. He's afraid of everything, and I'm not afraid of anything! He's a really serious student, and I'm, well, not serious at all.

Benny always helps me do my homework, and I always carry his briefcase for him. On him, it looks like a bookcase. And at recess, I always make sure he eats the food his mother sends for him, so that he'll grow big and strong. And you know, nobody ever makes fun of Benny for being so little and skinny. I think it's because they're scared it would make me mad.

This week was the first time I used my strength for real. Here's what happened:

In the hallway in our school, there's an enormous cabinet, with hundreds of books inside. Naturally, the principal doesn't allow anyone to climb on it, but there are a few wild kids in our school who are always fooling around and trying to climb up the sides of the book cabinet — don't ask me why.

The other day during recess, six kids were climbing on the cabinet at the same time, and all of a sudden the closet collapsed and fell over. All six of them, and a few other kids who were passing by, were trapped underneath.

All the teachers were up in the teachers' lounge at that moment, and the teacher on duty was out watching the kids playing in the school-yard. The boys under the closet were screaming and crying, but their voices sounded weak and muffled. It was terrible. All the other kids stood by in horror, and no one moved. I knew I had to act, and fast.

I just grabbed onto the whole side of that closet and with every ounce of strength I had, I started to lift it, with all those books flopping around. Somehow I found more strength to scream, "HELP! HELP!"

Two or three of the trapped boys started creeping out through the small space I had managed to make by lifting the closet. I felt as if my hands were being torn apart. That closet would have been too heavy even for a grown-up. I felt I was about to drop it, but I held on, knowing how much worse the kids underneath would be hurt if it fell again.

I was soaked with sweat, and I thought I was going to faint, when three of the teachers, who had heard my screams, came running over. All together, with all their strength, they managed to raise the closet higher. I crawled under it and pulled out some boys who couldn't climb out alone.

Afterwards, we found out that two of them had broken legs and the rest had terrible bruises. It was really a miracle that none of them were hurt worse than that.

The next day, the principal called an assembly for the whole school. He spoke about how dangerous it is for kids to get wild. He said how grateful to Hashem we should be that the day hadn't ended in real tragedy. And then he said that he wanted to mention one particular boy who was an example for the whole school, a boy who had strength, but used it only to do good. "All of you can learn from him how to use whatever gifts you have in order to do good for others," were his words.

Then the principal turned to me and said, "Yochai, you aren't the only strong boy in our school, but you're the one everybody — the teachers as well as the students — respects most. Do you know why? Because you use your brains more than your brawn, and because you have such a kind heart, that everyone benefits from your strength, and doesn't suffer from it."

Well, all the kids started clapping and cheering, and I really turned red. I didn't know what to do with myself. I mean, what were they making such a big deal about? I just did what I was supposed to do.

Out of the corner of my eye, I noticed that quiet little Benny had climbed up on a table to clap, and he was shouting louder than all the others: "Yochai! Yochai!" I laughed.

The next day, I went to school with Benny as usual, only this time he had to carry his own briefcase — and mine too. I couldn't carry anything: my hands were killing me! And you know why.

My name is Avremie and I'm in fourth grade.
Sometimes I worry. Once I remember worrying a lot.
At night I heard my mother calling all the big kids
in the family to another room. I was so worried.
What happened? What was she telling them? Maybe
something terrible happened and they weren't telling me.
I finally fell asleep and when I got up in the morning
my mother was in the kitchen and I saw that she was
happy. So I asked her and she told me that my brother was
engaged. So I realized that I didn't have to worry.

My name is chezzy.
For my tenth birthday, my parents gave
me gifts, and my grandparents gave me money.
I was so happy and I decided to take the
money and buy myself a present. When I left
the house I saw an old man dressed in rags
asking for tzedakah. I felt really sorry
for him and I wanted to give him my money
but my yetzer ha-ra didn't let me. It
convinced me that I should keep going to the
store and buy a present for myself.
When I got to the store, I looked at all the
games and I remembered the old man, and I just
couldn't buy anything so I left the store
and ran and ran, back to the old man,
and gave him my money, and I felt that I
did a good deed.

                     chezzy.

Little Sister, Big Problem

My name is Na'ama. I'm in fifth grade. I do well in school, my classmates like me, and I have some good friends. But I have a big problem, and it makes me miserable: my little sister.

You're probably thinking: A sister? Is a sister a problem?

Yes, sometimes a sister is a problem.

My sister Esti is in fourth grade, and the whole school knows her name. She's not quiet like me. She always has something to say — a bright remark, or a joke that makes everyone laugh. "She's really *something*!" That's what people say about Esti.

She also happens to have a talent for speaking. Last year she had the lead in the Purim play, and from then on, you heard her name wherever you went — the students and the teachers were all so impressed with her talent.

And in our family, too — all the uncles and aunts who come to visit us seem to be interested only in Esti. And it really hurts me.

I'm sure you're thinking: Oh, she's just jealous!

True. But you have to admit that it's a very hard thing for a girl when no one pays any attention to her, and everybody thinks the world of her little sister!

Don't think I talk about this. I've never told my mother. I'm only telling it to you. I never tell anybody how I really feel.

Anyway, all of this was *before*. Two days ago, I heard my parents talking to each other about me. Of course, they didn't know I was listening. This is what they said:

Mommy: "I get the feeling that Na'ama is very unhappy these days. I'm afraid she's jealous of Esti."

Daddy: "Jealous? What does she have to be jealous of?"

Mommy: "Well, she probably thinks that we think more of Esti than of her. You know how outgoing and popular Esti is. Na'ama is just a quieter personality. But if she only knew how I rely on her, she wouldn't be jealous! Personally, I think Esti has a wonderful talent for expressing herself, but I find Na'ama a much more serious and responsible child — and these are qualities which are far more important than being the center of attention. Esti actually has a lot to learn from Na'ama."

Daddy: "That's true. The greatest men and women among our people, the greatest Torah scholars and the most pious and famous women, were not necessarily those who made a name for themselves as children. On the contrary, diligence, dependability and a serious attitude — these are the qualities which lead to greatness in a Jewish woman."

And the conversation went on like that....

Well, hearing that made me really happy, but on the other hand, I'm confused. Because even though I know it's true what they said — I still have a feeling I would rather be like Esti!

What do you kids think?

"Sorry!"

My name is Shuki. My story goes back two years, to when I was in fourth grade. At recess each morning, every class in the school would stampede outside, and try to be the first to claim the schoolyard for their game. Most of the time, the bigger kids — the seventh- or eighth-graders — got the yard first and we little kids had to make do with one of the corners... Once in a long while, though, we would get there first and grab the main court for ourselves.

One day, the teacher let us out a minute before the bell rang, and we ran like crazy to be the first class out to the yard. We started our game right away.

Suddenly, a big group of kids from the seventh grade ran out and started playing right where we were playing, just as if we weren't even there. We protested, we yelled at them, we threatened them, but they just ignored us.

I decided to take action. At an opportune moment, I grabbed the ball they were playing with, and threw it over the fence....

David, a seventh-grader, ran outside to get it, and when he came back with the ball, his face was bright red with anger. Sparks flew out of his eyes, and he gave me a really scary look. He came closer to me and then he took the ball and slammed it straight at me.

All I remember is that the world turned upside down, and then went black. I was out cold.

When I came to, the principal was bent over me. He looked really worried. He and one of the teachers carried me into the office and gently washed my face. I realized that I could hardly see at all out of one eye. It dawned on me that I had been hurt badly.

Sure enough, an ambulance came right away and I was taken to a hospital where my father met me, looking pale and worried. I tried to smile at him, but I don't think I did such a good job.... They did some tests, and then they decided that I had a severe hemorrhage in my eye — whatever *that* meant. My father whispered with the doctors, still looking very worried, and then they wheeled me off to treat my eye.

Afterwards, they put a gigantic bandage on my eye, and they even bandaged the other one, because they were afraid I would strain it.

I fell asleep, and I slept for an entire day. When I woke up, I could feel the warmth of the sun on my face, but I couldn't see a thing. It felt so strange. So this is what it feels like to be blind, I thought.

I became aware of a rustling sound next to my bed. "Who's there?" I asked. No answer. I asked again, "Who's that next to me?" All I heard were footsteps hurrying away, and then silence.

A few minutes later, my father came into the room. He asked me how I was, and he got me ready for the doctor's rounds. A few days passed. Each day, in the late afternoon, I felt a mysterious presence beside my bed, one that didn't speak or make any sound.

On the fourth day, I had an idea. When I felt that the hour was approaching, I carefully lifted the bandage which covered my good eye just a drop so that I could see what was going on. Sure enough, at the usual time, the familiar, hesitant footsteps sounded and in walked... David! He sat down next to me, and I could see his face through the bandage. He looked so sad, and full of concern. He looked very closely at my swollen face, and his own eyes filled with tears. He had no idea, of course, that I was watching him.

I was remembering how furious those same eyes looked just before he threw the ball at me.

He is really sorry, I thought. But if he had thought before, the accident that made me suffer all this would not have happened.

In a harsh voice, I said, "I would like my guest to leave the room, immediately!"

David was stunned, and his face got red. He leaned over my bed, took a deep breath, and said, "It's me, David. I want to tell you I'm sorry, to ask you to forgive me. I feel terrible about what happened." After a moment's hesitation, he said, "I acted like a *rasha* and I am so ashamed."

I did not answer. I kept quiet.

"Do you forgive me, Shuki?" David's voice trembled.

He stared at the floor, and didn't seem to know what to do with himself. He started walking out of the room. Before he reached the door, I called him back. "David!" He stopped, turned around, and came back with measured steps.

"Sit down, David," I said to him. He sat, and it was quiet for a little while. Then I said, "I forgive you."

"Thank you," was all he could reply. After a few minutes, he got up and said, "I'm going, Shuki." Again, he started toward the door. Again I called him back. "David!" He turned his head, and I asked, "Will you be coming tomorrow too?" He smiled and said that he would.

The next day, David came at his usual time, which was right after school was over. We started talking and I realized that, even though he was in seventh grade, and I was only in fourth, he was treating me like an equal, and telling me all about things that were happening in his class. I told him things too, and I tried to make them interesting and not babyish so I wouldn't bore him.

My father came in and found us talking to each other. He looked at me and smiled. "Did you work it out?" he asked. Together, we answered, "Yes!"

Later, after David had gone home, I asked my father, "How do you know who this is?" He told me that on the very day that the whole thing happened, David appeared, trembling and crying with regret and pain, and asked if he could visit me. From that day on, he had sat by to watch my recovery. He had asked my father not to tell me who the mystery guest was, and my father had agreed.

Within two weeks, my eye had healed, and I was back in school.

Ever since, David and I have been really good friends — inseparable.

A year passed. I was in fifth grade and David was in eighth. We started learning together on Shabbos. First, David would review whatever

Gemara I was learning that week, and later he started teaching me what he had learned that week. In the end, we decided to learn a different Gemara altogether, one that neither of us was learning in school.

Our friendship grew stronger and stronger. All our friends got used to seeing us together.

David is finishing eighth grade now and he'll be going off to a yeshiva in a different city. I'll be in sixth grade and I don't know what I'll do without him. Of course, we decided to stay in touch by writing to each other, and we'll keep telling each other what's going on with our learning and our friends.

It'll be hard for me, though, to be separated from such a good friend. My only consolation is that the friendship itself will never be broken.

The main lesson of my story and its happy ending is this: that saying "I'm sorry" is a very important thing. David has told me how hard it was for him to say it. And saying "I forgive you" is no easier, believe me. But those difficulties were nothing, when you think what we gained by saying "I'm sorry" and "I forgive you." We each gained a real friend forever.

The Sharpshooter

My name is Ruvi. I'm in fifth grade, in Bnei Brak.

I'm just a regular kid. I'm not an especially great student, but my grades are okay.

There would never have been any way the whole school would know my name, except for the gogos.

I think everyone must know what a gogo is, but if you don't, I'll tell you. It's an apricot pit, and all the kids collect them and play games with them. Here in Bnei Brak we call them gogos. In Yerushalayim, they call them ajous, and in Haifa — actually, I don't know what they call them in Haifa.

When I was just in second grade, I started to notice how exciting the gogo games in the schoolyard were. One kid after another would hold a can with holes punched in the top, calling: "Who wants to shoot?" One day I asked an older boy what the rules of the game were.

65

He had a great big fancy can in his hand, and he explained: "You stand over there and you aim your gogo at my can. If you get one into the big hole, you win four gogos, and if you get it into the smaller hole, you win ten."

"What about this hole?" I asked, pointing to a very small hole, just about the size of a gogo.

"Forget that! In your whole life, you'll never manage to get one in there," he answered scornfully. "That one would get you a hundred gogos." I asked him to lend me a gogo, so that I could try my hand.

I stepped back a bit from the can, aimed for that tiny hole, and — whoopee! — the gogo went right through it into the can.

Suddenly, there was quiet all around us. The boy was shocked. I quickly said, "That was *your* gogo. So you don't owe me anything." The boy breathed a sigh of relief, and I walked off with a title: "Sharpshooter."

It seems that I have a very good eye for distance. By now I've accumulated a large collection of gogos, all because of my well-aimed shots. But after playing for only a few weeks, I realized that gogos are not important. "It's only a childish game," I thought. Still, I kept on playing.

Do you know why? Because I discovered that through this game, you can find out a lot about the character of the kids who are playing.

If I play with a kid and win, and he gets mad, and throws the gogos at me, then I know that kid is an angry type and a sore loser.

And if another one smiles and says, "You sure are making me poor, Sharpshooter," then I can see that, even though it hurts to lose, this guy knows how to lose gracefully.

I can also tell which kids are honest — those who admit things like, "The can moved while you were aiming, so you get another chance." I usually let it go, and even give them an extra gogo as a reward for their honesty.

Then there's the other kind, kids who aren't really honest, and are always accusing the winner of standing too close, or making up any excuse they can think of — anything, as long as they don't have to pay up.

Once I told a kid like that, "You know, when you grow up — unless you change — people will never believe you. Gogos for us kids are just like money for grown-ups. If a kid can't be straight and honest in the gogo business — then he's not going to be honest in real business when he grows up."

Even now, I still like to play. The other kids know that I never ever lie, and that my word can always be depended on. Sometimes, I'm asked to be the referee in their games.

I'll end this by telling you about something that happened to me this week.

I was outside at recess, when I noticed two kids with cans — one was a seventh-grader, and the other, a third-grader. Lots of kids were lining up to shoot, but all of them were choosing the seventh-grader, a strong, loud-mouthed boy. Sure enough, that kid had a huge pile of gogos, while the younger boy sat alone at the edge of the schoolyard, looking sadly at all the kids on line.

I happened to have a bag on me with about a hundred gogos in it, so I went over to the quiet little kid, and started throwing mine at his can. I pretended to aim, but I really didn't even try. I wanted him to have as big a gogo collection as possible.

I threw about fifty gogos, and lost them all. Meanwhile, all the kids in the school were crowding around to see the Sharpshooter losing for a change. I didn't care. I just kept raining my gogos in the direction of that happy little kid.

Then, when I had only one gogo left in my hand, I turned to the other can, the one belonging to that big kid who was so proud of his collection. Somehow, all the kids who had aimed for his can had lost. I took very careful aim with my one gogo and threw it straight into that little hole that wins one hundred.

Silence. Every boy held his breath.

In the end, I let him off too, and walked away empty-handed. You see, for me, gogos are nothing but a game. What I really wanted to do was teach them all to care about the feelings of other kids, and to show that you can sometimes give in to someone even if he doesn't deserve it. That's the biggest pleasure of all, in my opinion.

Beauty

My name is Leah.

I don't like to look in the mirror, because the face that looks back at me is not very nice to look at. I'm ugly.

I wasn't always like this. I have a picture of myself from when I was five years old. I was a cute little girl with pretty eyes.

But not long after that picture was taken — so my mother tells me — a fire broke out in our house when I was asleep in my room. Everything in the house was destroyed, and, by a miracle, the firemen managed to get me out. But by then, my clothing had caught fire, and my face got badly burned.

I spent nearly a whole year in the hospital. The doctors worked hard just to keep me alive. And they succeeded. They saved my life.

But there is one thing they couldn't do. They couldn't get me to look normal again. My face looks just awful, scary, like one gigantic burn.

The only thing that remained from my cute face is two eyes. My mother says they're beautiful.

Now I'm ashamed to walk down the street. I always think everybody is looking at me. The people who know what happened to me whisper to each other when I pass. The ones who don't know just pity me. There are even some who laugh at me, and that hurts a lot.

Isn't it enough that my outside was damaged? Do I also have to get so hurt inside my heart and soul?

I think a lot about beauty these days. It's nothing more than an outside wrapping — it doesn't show anything about what's inside a person.

I notice that kids act much nicer to other kids who are nice-looking. Even if those kids don't have kind hearts and even if they do things that hurt others. But to a kid like me, who wouldn't hurt a fly, they don't pay any attention at all. They don't ask me to join their games, and worst of all, they act *mean* to girls like me, and just stay away.

Why do I deserve this? Did I ever hurt them?

If I looked like everybody else, I would thank Hashem every day for making me so fortunate, and I would be so nice to kids who looked ugly.

But all those kids who've always been fine — *they* never went through this feeling, and they don't know what it's like. They act as though I'm ugly *inside*.

I'm writing to all of you out there: Please try to get to know me! Please try to ignore my terrible problem! I can still play and laugh just exactly like you, and a kid like me also deserves friends.

If you have a kind heart, dear reader, I'm sure my words will reach it.

S.T.A.L.K.

My name is Yishai. I live in Yerushalayim. I'm not a quiet kid. I have lots of energy, and I like to play and to run around, and sometimes I, well, get into a little trouble.

I also read a lot. My favorites are the books about groups of kids that get together and investigate things, solve mysteries, and have exciting adventures. They remind me of myself.

One day I decided that I would start my own group of kids to investigate all kinds of things. I got my friends together — Yossi, Shlomo, and Uzi — and we established S.T.A.L.K.: the Society to Aid Less-fortunate Kids. We decided that our job would be to protect children who needed help and to try to do things for them.

One day in school, our teacher told us about certain gentiles who would take Jewish children away in order to convert them to other religions. These people are called missionaries. Well, we

73

didn't exactly bother to find out whether this kind of thing still goes on. We just decided that it sounded like an exciting idea for our first project: we would hunt down these missionaries and keep those unfortunate children away from them.

We started by making up special badges. On each badge were the letters S.T.A.L.K. The rest of the class didn't know what was going on. And, of course, none of us said a word to anyone outside the group about our secret, after-school activities. Shlomo brought a walkie-talkie, so that we could follow any suspicious-looking people and report back to each other. Yossi brought a camera, so we could take pictures to show the police.

Not far from our school, there's an old, neglected building. Almost no one ever seems to go near it, but sometimes a mysterious old lady comes out of the second-floor apartment, and later returns to it.

We began to suspect that this was a missionary house.

We sprang into action. We set up lookout points from where we could watch the house. To our surprise, after two hours of watching the place, we saw a car pull up to the house. Two men got out and entered the building. "Shlomo," I announced over the walkie-talkie, "it's Yishai.

I'm going to follow those men."

"What's the matter with you?" Shlomo relayed back to me. "It's dangerous!"

But I was determined to go after them, no matter what. I went into the building and started up the stairs. Suddenly, I heard a voice: "Where are you?" I ran down quickly and hid behind the staircase. Then I heard, "I'm over here. Come on, let's pull this trunk out together." Then I heard the sound of something heavy being dragged. I heard the old lady's voice asking something, and a man's voice answering: "The trunk will reach it's destination. You have nothing to worry about. No one will know a thing."

Immediately I understood everything: Inside the trunk was a Jewish child, and these people wanted to kidnap him! I pressed the broadcast button on the walkie-talkie so that my friends could hear everything, and also so that they wouldn't be able to broadcast anything to me, and give away my hiding-place.

Sure enough, the trunk thumped down the stairs, and the two men loaded it into their car and sped off. Yossi quickly snapped a picture of them. We contacted the police immediately and told them the whole story. But they refused to take us seriously! They just smiled and said, "Okay, kids — now go out and play."

I realized that we would have to act on our

own. I told Yossi and Shlomo: "I'll climb up to the window of the apartment to see if there are any other kidnapped children in there."

"Aren't you scared?" Uzi asked.

"Not at all," I said, even though I was trembling with fear.

The boys lifted me up on their shoulders. I held on to the drainpipe and started climbing. I soon found myself at the second floor window. It was closed, but not locked, and I saw that it opened inward. Very slowly, I started to push it in. But suddenly, I saw a terrifying sight: A very old man with a white face was standing there, absolutely still, opposite the window I was looking in, and he was staring straight at me! A cry of terror burst out of my throat, I lost my hold, and I fell into the room.

I opened my eyes to find myself lying in the darkened room, and who was standing over me, but — you guessed it — the old lady! I started to yell, "Help!" and she tried to calm me down. "Don't worry, young man, I'll help you."

"No! No, you won't," I yelled. "You just want to kidnap me the way you kidnapped the other boy in that trunk!"

The lady was amazed to hear my words. "Wh– what?" she started to ask, and then she burst out laughing. "What? A kidnapped boy?" she asked, trying to control her laughter.

Then she said to me, very gently: "Come, I want to show you something." She led me to a room filled with toys and children's clothing. "Do you see all this?" she asked. "These clothes and toys are meant for needy children whose parents don't have enough money to buy them such things. I collect all these things here, and every few days two men who help me come to pick up a trunkful or two."

Then she showed me a thank-you letter from a *tzedakah* organization. It even mentioned that all the things were given out without the people knowing where they came from. But I still wasn't entirely convinced. "Well, what about that white-faced old man that I saw?" I asked. The woman was silent for a minute, thinking. Then her eyes lit up. "I think I know who you mean," she said.

She brought me back to the room I had fallen into, and I walked in after her, very suspicious. But when I saw what had scared me so badly, I had to laugh out loud. On the wall, directly opposite the window, hung a life-sized portrait of an old man.

"That's my husband, may he rest in peace," said the old woman in a soft voice. "It's in his memory that I started this project to help unfortunate children."

Well, now I understood everything.

Suddenly, my walkie-talkie crackled to life. "Yishai, Yishai," said a worried voice, "what's happening? Do you need help?"

The old lady and I started to laugh together. Then I answered, "The members of S.T.A.L.K. are cordially invited to come upstairs."

My friends came up very hesitantly. The old lady and I then explained exactly what kind of activity was taking place in this house.

Ever since, S.T.A.L.K. has been awfully busy. Every week we go around to the homes of the kids in our school, and collect their old clothing and toys for less-fortunate kids. Then we take the stuff to that wonderful lady, and she hands them over to good men who give them out to people who need them without revealing where they came from.

In the end, you see, we're doing exactly what we planned to do from the start. We're the Society to Aid Less-fortunate Kids.

The Scholarly Inventor

My name is Rafi. Everybody calls me "Rafi the Inventor." And not for nothing. I happen to know how to invent things.

For example, I invented a free telephone. I found the receivers from two old phones in the street one day, and I took them apart. Inside each one, I discovered two round metal discs with holes in them — one disc in the mouthpiece and one in the earpiece. I rigged them up and connected them with a long electrical wire. I put one set in my house, and I drew the wire across the hill that separates my house from my friend Mordy's house. Since then, Mordy and I can talk whenever we want on our own phone, for free.

In my room, I have a garbage can that I open by pulling a string near my bed, and in my drawer there's a motor that I built myself. I can hook it up to an airplane that I also built myself, and — believe it or not — the airplane actually flies for a little while, until the motor slows down and it falls. I'm working on that problem, and — God willing — I'll solve it.

On my way home from school, I always have my eyes peeled for new finds. By the time I get home, my pockets are stuffed with all kinds of exciting things: little wheels from toy cars, springs of all sizes, broken pens, and bent antennas. I sit down in my room, finish my homework fast, and then I devote my full attention to the day's finds and to making new inventions.

During recess I'm busy selling my inventions. The price is a bar or two of chocolate, depending on the importance of the invention. One of the things I sell, for example, is a metal box which has copper buttons you can press to make different sounds.

To tell the truth, it's not so much that I want the chocolate, as that I enjoy seeing other people use my inventions. But if I gave them away for free, the whole school would grab them, and I really don't want that.

I mean, as it is, the teachers give me a hard time, even though I'm considered one of the best students. I always finish tests first, and I get As without any trouble at all. Still, they're not so thrilled with me, and they're right. I sometimes get an urge to work on my inventions during class, and a teacher may catch me fastening a propellor to a battery with some electrical wire. Or, a teacher may decide to ask me to empty out my bulging pockets, and I'll unload a gigantic collection. Like: three wheels from a toy bus, three batteries, two rolls of electric wire, wood scraps for building a car, and a little container of glue that sticks your fingers together if you don't watch out. My teacher once found a whole sink faucet in my pocket....

One day, my teacher called me over after class. "Sit down, Rafi," he said. "I want to talk to you." He was quiet for a few minutes and his face looked so serious that I began to get nervous. "I don't want to spoil the pleasure you get from all your inventions," he began, "but it seems to me you are taking this a bit too far. Sometimes I think that you care more about any old piece of wire than anything else. What's happened to your enthusiasm for your studies?"

I didn't answer. How could I explain that my love of inventing things was simply greater than my love of learning? Of course I still loved learning, but....

"Let me tell you something, Rafi," he said. "Hashem blesses each of us with different talents. Your gift of finding things and putting them together to invent something is a blessing. But think: to be a *talmid chacham* you have to be a kind of inventor too. You use a piece of knowledge here, a part there, and put it all together to create a new insight."

I smiled. I'd never thought of that before! But yes, it's true — I thought of how *Chazal* always help us see how things fit together....

"And you know, Rafi, that doesn't mean you have to give up your talent for inventing *things* too. You know, there are lots of inventions that help Jews to observe the mitzvos — like a Shabbos clock, or computers that check *sifrei Torah.*

"But let's put first things first. First, apply your gifts to learning Torah and really understanding the *halachos.* And then when you're grown up, you can apply your learning to inventing things that help people to observe the mitzvos."

As I walked home, I didn't look around for pieces of things — I just thought, and thought.

When I got home I went into my room and closed the door.

On the bookshelf opposite my door, the gold letters of the words *Bava Metziah* seemed to smile out at me from the binding. Suddenly I knew my teacher was right. I knew what was important for me to do now, more than anything else. I took the Gemara off the shelf, and sat down to learn.

The next day, I went back to school as if nothing unusual had happened. I continued building things of course (mostly at home), but my friends realized that somehow I had changed.

These days, fewer and fewer kids are calling me "Rafi the Inventor," and I find that some have even started calling me "Rafi the Scholar." You know, I think I like the sound of that even more.

My Friend from the Grocery

My name is Avichai. I live in Petach Tikvah, and I go to a school called Sha'arei Torah, which is not so close to my house. It takes me about twenty minutes to walk there every morning.

On the way, I have to cross a busy main street that separates the neighborhood where I live from the neighborhood where my school is. I wait a few minutes at the traffic light until it's okay for me cross.

What I do is, I leave my house at half past seven, and I get to the street at twenty minutes to eight. I wait five minutes for the light to change, and then I cross, and get to school at five to eight.

I've been doing this for years — since first grade! Every day I pass the same places at exactly the same time. I mean, if you come by at twenty to eight, you'll see me standing at the traffic light. At a quarter to eight, you'll see me walking across to the other side, on my way to the school.

Why am I telling you all this?

It's because of the man I call "my friend from the grocery store." He walks in the opposite direction every morning. He walks toward the neighborhood I come from. We meet in front of the grocery store on the other side of the street. Now, we must both be very exact people, since we seem to leave our houses each morning at exactly the same time, and that's why we pass each other at precisely the same spot every day. Our "meeting" lasts less than a minute, because each of us is hurrying in his own direction.

For months, we would pass each other without even saying hello. After all, we didn't know each other. But with time, I got used to the idea that near that grocery, every single morning, rain or shine, I would always see that old man walking toward me.

One morning, I left my house as usual on my way to school, and as soon as I started walking, I saw the old man coming in my direction! I quickly looked at my watch, thinking that if he were here already, I must be late. But the man smiled at me and said, "Don't worry, I left early today!" I laughed and went on my way.

The next day, I passed him as always at the grocery store. This time, I nodded a hello.

As the days passed, we found ourselves greeting each other like old friends. Once, I saw him walking with an open Mishnah in his hands. As he passed me, he quoted something that he knew I would understand. I just smiled back at him.

From then on, we began exchanging short greetings — always without stopping, of course. Like: "I have a test today." "Good luck!" Or: "I have a new grandson." "*Mazal tov!*" Once, he said, "My foot hurts today," and I shot "Be well!" in his direction. Everything was said while we each continued walking quickly.

We went on this way for half a year. I still didn't know his name or where he lived, but I knew that I had a friend, and I felt somehow that he was a very special friend. It's true that our friendship was kind of "passing," but it was a dependable, smiley, pleasant friendship. "My friend from the grocery store," I called him, because I didn't know any other name for him.

Walking past him every day, I started to pick up little things, like the fact that he's a teacher, for example. How do I know? Once he called out, "Take a coat, I have a lot of students with colds!" "Thanks!" I cried after him. He nodded

his head without turning back.

He also knows some things about me. He knows when my birthday is. I told him. The next day, he gave me a present, walking by! He just handed me a beautiful *Sefer Tehillim* as he passed, and kept on walking. Once, he handed me a little note which said, "Pray for Refael *ben* Miriam." I didn't know anything about the name except that it must be someone close to my friend. So I organized reciting *Tehillim* in all the classes. I said mine from the *Sefer Tehillim* he gave me, which I guard very carefully.

Yesterday was the last day of school.

I walked to school and saw him as always, walking toward me. When I came up to him, I said, "See you next year!"

And then something strange happened. The man did not keep on going. He stopped. I realized that he must have something more to say to me. So I also stood still.

"It looks like we won't be meeting at the grocery store anymore," he said softly. "I won't be teaching next year. My students don't listen to me anymore. They think that since I'm an old man, they can act up in my class. So I decided that it was time for me to retire from teaching."

I was shocked. "How could it be that children would give up such a nice teacher?" I asked.

He just shook his head a bit, looking embarrassed. His eyes were very sad.

I stood there and didn't say anything. I felt my own eyes filling up with tears. My heart ached — it really hurt.

"Well, *I'm* not giving you up," I told my friend — whose name I didn't even know. "Could you just learn with me — be my *chavrusa*?"

His face lit up. "Of course," he said. "I would like that very much — even though I don't even know your name!"

That's the story. I gained a very special teacher, that a whole class lost.

Every Shabbos I learn with him in a shul that's not far from the grocery store, every week at exactly the same time.

Even though we know each other's names now, I think that for me he'll always be "my friend from the grocery."

The Businessman

My name is Aryeh. I'm in sixth grade.

I'm a pretty good student, but that's not what I'm known for. Everyone calls me "Aryeh the Businessman."

Are you wondering why?

It's because I'm always thinking up ways to make some money. Once, when collecting bottle caps was very popular, I got a bright idea. I prepared a hundred small sandwich bags, filled them each with ten bottle caps, and tied each one with a yellow ribbon.

During recess, I sold the bags for twenty cents apiece. Figure it out: a hundred times twenty cents is twenty dollars — all of it earned from bottle caps, which I got for free from the corner candy store!

That's just one example. I keep coming up with new ideas and making money out of them.

At the beginning of this year, I had a real

brainstorm. I bought ten different greeting cards for Rosh Hashanah. Then I went to a store that has a copy machine, and made eight photocopies of each Rosh Hashanah card. I went home and carefully pasted the copies onto sheets of oak tag. I had eight sheets of oak tag, with ten different greeting cards on each one. Then I made more photocopies of the sheets of oak tag, and had several hundred greeting cards altogether.

The next morning, I arrived in school with my stock. I hung up a sign that said: SPECIAL SALE OF *SHANAH TOVAH* CARDS DURING RECESS IN THE SIXTH GRADE CLASSROOM. What a sensation it made! All the cards were sold on the first day. There are six hundred kids in the school, and lots of them figured it was smarter to pay half a dollar for eight cards than to go to a store and buy cards for a dollar each. Some of them even bought a few sheets of oak tag.

And I went home with a hundred and fifty dollars!!

Well, the next day, I made double the amount, and those were also grabbed up. That day I came home with three hundred dollars. With four hundred and fifty dollars in my little bank, I couldn't believe how rich I was!

I kept it up, and as the days passed, business got better and better. The word had spread, and kids from other schools started coming to buy my cards. And I just kept earning more and more money.

During class time, my mind was constantly on my business. I was always calculating how many more copies to make, how much the cost would be, and what my profit would be. I was so involved in my long columns of figures that sometimes when the teacher called on me, I didn't even know what the subject was.

During one recess, with sales in full swing and kids lined up outside the room, the teacher suddenly appeared beside me. Some of the kids got nervous and ran off. Then a few more left, and then the rest disappeared, and I found myself alone with the teacher.

"Well, well, Aryeh," the teacher said. "Now I see why your marks have gone down! Your head is full of business deals, so how can you learn?"

He picked up one of the sheets of oak tag and looked at it. As he studied it more closely, his face darkened. The longer he looked, the angrier he got. He raised his eyebrows, and asked me sharply: "Tell me, did you ask permission to photocopy all these greeting cards?"

"Permission? From whom?" I didn't know what he meant.

"From the person who designed and produced the cards," he replied. "He invested a

lot of time, work, and money in the produc-
tion of these cards, you know. And then you
come along and buy *one*, and make hundreds
of copies, and instead of paying him for them all
— people pay you! Does that seem fair to you?"

I was stunned. "Oh! How is it that I never
thought of that?" I wondered. I realized right
away that had I not done this copying, a lot
of the kids would have gone to the stores and
bought the cards there. The man who had made
them would have earned the profit.

"You know, it's as if I stole from him!" I told
the teacher, bitterly ashamed. "What should I
do now?"

"I think you have to return the money to the
one you stole it from," was his answer.

That afternoon, I went back to the card store,
and I asked the storekeeper for the phone number of the manufacturer of the Rosh Hashanah
cards. He looked at me suspiciously, but he gave
it to me.

I went home and, with a trembling hand, I
dialed the number.

The voice that answered sounded like that
of an older man. I told him my name and, of
course, he had no idea why a boy named Aryeh
was calling him. In a shaky voice, I explained
to him what I was calling about. He listened to
me, and from time to time he interrupted me to

ask a question. I could hear the surprise in his voice.

After I finished telling him the whole story, he asked for my number, and he said he'd think about it and call me back later on.

That evening the phone rang. My father picked it up. "Yes, I am his father," I heard him say. Then he was silent as he listened to what the caller had to say.

His face seemed to get sterner and angrier by the minute.

The conversation ended with some words of apology from my father, and his agreement to some suggestion which the caller had made.

My father replaced the receiver and gave me a long hard look. "Now I understand the sharp drop in your schoolwork lately," he said, and I burst into tears. He waited till I had calmed down and then he said: "The fact that you went to the man yourself shows me that you really do regret what happened with all your heart, and that you didn't intend to do anything wrong.

"I know that you enjoy being the 'businessman.' But you also know that there are things which are far more important. Most important of all is remembering that the Torah is worth more than any sum on earth, as in the verse 'Your Torah is more precious to me than thousands of gold and silver coins.' I am very sad to have to say, Aryeh, that it often seems as if you forget this, because your 'business deals' get in the way. Something that should be secondary has become the main thing in your life.

"And as for all that money you made," said my father, "the man says he is willing to forgo it and to forgive you — but on one condition: Half the money must go to *tzedakah* and the other half must be put in the bank until your wedding day. At that time, you will be permitted to use it, but only if you are a real *lamdan.*"

My father went on to explain that the kind and understanding man had told him, "If your son uses that sharp head of his to learn Torah, then the money can be his wedding gift. If not, it must be returned to me." My father looked me straight in the eye, and, after a moment, I nodded my agreement.

I know this whole story may seem unreal to you, but you should know that, as a result of these things, I started to concentrate on my Torah study, and to forget all about business! Now I really feel, deep in my heart, that Torah is more precious to me than gold or silver could ever be.

After the incident, the principal went around to all the classes in our school and announced that from now on, no business whatsoever could be transacted on school premises.

Not all the kids in the school knew why he made the rule, so I volunteered to explain it. Business — I told them — is for grown-ups. When kids try to get into it, it just takes them away from learning. Or, even worse, it can get them into big trouble, the way it did with me.

Nighttime Is Scary

My name is Rivky. I'm eight, and I'm in third grade.

I've never been a girl with problems, really. I mean, I'm a good student, I help my mother at home with the housework, and I take care of my little brother and sisters. I do my homework, play a lot, and everything's been fine, all in all.

But I did have one problem: nights. Every night, after finishing my homework and helping my mother get my brother and sisters into pajamas and to bed, I would lie down in my bed, say the *Shema* and close my eyes. And that was when, very slowly and softly, fear would start to fill my heart. I can't tell you what I was afraid of — maybe it was the dark, maybe that scary quiet of nighttime. I don't know. I just know I was afraid. I tried opening the shutters, and I tried closing them, but it didn't help. Somehow the fear had set up camp inside my room.

Even when my parents left a small light on, the fear kept me from falling asleep — in my own room. When I started going into my parents' room just about every night, and asking my mother if I could sleep with her in her bed, I could fall asleep in two minutes.

Every night, I would make up my mind all over again: "Tonight I won't be afraid!" Then I would lie there, waiting... Every small noise outside sounded to me like burglars trying to get in the window. At one point I called my father and he came into my room, opened the shutters, and showed me it was only a cat playing with an empty soda can. He tried to explain to me that the night doesn't have to be a scary thing — it's the time when people who work all day are sleeping, and when everything around us is at rest. "Why should you think something bad will happen during these quiet, restful hours?" he asked.

But it didn't help me one bit. My fears just grew stronger. When I wasn't dreaming about burglars, I was seeing imaginary, mysterious creatures that seemed to be coming toward me in the dark. Then I would rush straight for my mother's bed.

One morning, my father and my mother and I sat down together to figure out what could be done. All of us knew my fears were foolish, but the fact was that I was really scared!

My parents said they understood, but that at my age, sleeping in my mother's bed was something that had to stop. "You're eight years old already," they said. "You're really too old to keep doing this, Rivky — don't you agree?"

I did.

"I have an idea," my mother said. "Every time you get scared, you can come to me as usual, but instead of getting into my bed, *I'll* come back to *your* room with you and I'll sit in the chair near your bed for a while, until you fall asleep. Let's see if that helps."

The idea appealed to me. I mean, I didn't want to keep acting like a baby. So that's what we did. When I couldn't sleep because something frightened me, or if I woke up from a scary dream, I called my mother. She would sit down near my bed and calm me down. Sometimes she'd turn on the light and give me a book, and I'd read till I got tired and fell asleep.

One night, my mother thought I had fallen asleep. She kissed me gently on the forehead, turned off the light, and tiptoed out. She didn't know that I was still awake, and I didn't call out to her. Well, I started getting scared as usual, but then I told myself: Wait a minute! You felt so safe just now, and you weren't afraid of any-thing, just because Imma was sitting here. And now, she's only in the next room — why should you be afraid?

So I closed my eyes and I started thinking about the *pesukim* we say in *Kerias Shema*: "Hashem is with me, I will not fear." And, "You, Hashem, are a shield before me." And when I thought about "the angel who saves me from all evil," a warm feeling spread through me. I felt that I kind of knew that Hashem is really with me always, that He sent a good angel to watch over me, and that He sent my father and my mother, who are right nearby.

I fell asleep!

The next morning, I ran to my mother in the kitchen and said, "You know, Imma, I think you'll be able to sleep in peace from now on! My fears are not going to bother me anymore."

And so it was. Ever since that night, I feel bigger and stronger and freer of all those silly fears. And if any of you get scared at night, don't be ashamed — it happens to a lot of us. Just tell yourself over and over that you aren't alone, that Hashem is always with you, protecting you. Then you'll be able to get rid of your fears and stop sleeping with your parents — and you'll feel grown up, and happy. Try it!

My name is Gila.

Maybe you won't believe that when I was seven I was the babysitter for my little brothers and sister when my parents had to go to work at night. Once when I was watching them, I heard knocking at the door and I asked, who's there? and nobody answered me, and I got so scared my heart was pounding. The man said, OPEN UP! and just then I opened and it was my uncle. I sure calmed down when I saw it was my uncle and not some stranger, and my uncle asked me where my mother and father were and I told him. When my uncle left, I had to calm my sister down and then my father came home and I told him the whole thing, and he said I wasn't supposed to open the door if I didn't know who it was I cried and then my father made me feel better and I fell asleep.

Jumping Jack

My name is Asher.

Even though I'm a good student, some of my teachers aren't very pleased with me. They call me "Jumping Jack."

I always get the highest marks on tests, and when the teacher asks a question, I always know the answer. And I sometimes ask questions that the teacher says great Rabbis asked too!

But they still aren't very happy with me. Are you wondering why? Well, the problem is that I can't sit still for more than five minutes at a time. I just *can't.*

The Mishnah teacher spends a whole hour explaining something to the class that I understood after the first five minutes. And then I have nothing to do.

And in Gemara class, it's even worse. I'm in a dream world there. I learn Gemara with my father every night, exactly the way we do in school. So when the teacher explains it again, it just seems babyish to me.

So what do I do? I get out of my seat and take a little walk... anything — I mean, I'm sick of sitting and dreaming the whole day. And when I'm not walking around, I find other ways to pass the time: I tear up paper into tiny pieces, or take apart my watch and put it back together, or make paper airplanes.

I happen to be a great paper-airplane maker. I once discovered that if you make a small paper airplane, it falls down pretty quickly, so from then on, I started building them with very long wings. And if you make sure that the folds are exact, and very small and pressed down hard, then the airplane stays in the air for a long time!

One day, I was trying out one of these great airplanes right in the middle of class. Of course, I didn't mean to disturb the class! It's just that I was so wrapped up in my airplane, that I completely forgot there was a class going on....

But the teacher got really mad, and he sent me to the principal's office. The principal sent me home with a letter to my parents. My father was very upset.

I don't like to make my father sad, so I really try to listen in class. But it just doesn't work. I already know just about everything the teacher is saying — and so there's nothing for me to do in class. It's all so boring.

One day, after class ended, the teacher called me into the teachers' lounge. "Look, Asher," he said, "you are probably the most gifted boy in the class, but I am not pleased with your behavior, and you know it."

What could I say?

I was fiddling with a sheet of paper at the time, folding it without paying attention to what I was doing. The teacher took it from me gently and made a few quick folds in it himself. Suddenly, there was a paper boat in his hands! "You see, Asher?" he said, "I know how to do this too. The question is, what good will come of it?"

I kept quiet.

The teacher looked into my eyes and said, "I know what your problem is. When you get to school in the morning, everything that I will be teaching that day is already in your head. So you feel that there's nothing more for you to learn in class that day. Right?"

I nodded.

"Well, if that's the case, why come to school at all? Stay home and do something useful!"

I couldn't think of anything to say.

"Think about the problem," said the teacher, "and maybe you'll be able to come up with a solution." He stood up, patted me on my shoulder, and walked away.

When I got home, I sat at my desk trying to think of a solution, and I couldn't find one.

In the evening, my father came home and said, as usual, "Asher, are you ready to learn?" And then, all of a sudden, the idea came to me!

"Abba," I said, "Maybe we could learn a different Gemara — one we aren't learning in school?"

My father was surprised. "Why don't you want to learn the one you're learning in school?"

"Because if I learn the Gemara with you first, then I'm just bored in class. Maybe we can review it a little, Abba, and then learn something different." My father was very happy about my idea. That night we started to learn a new Gemara.

What can I tell you, kids? It really has made a difference. Ever since that day, I sit in class and soak up the teacher's words. Because the material is new, I find it really interests me. It's so nice to be able to listen along with everyone else and to realize that my teacher has a very interesting way of teaching.

Now, don't think I've given up paper-airplane building. I just manage to find other times for that activity. But during class, I'm too busy — learning!

Nechama's Secret

My name is Channy, and I'm in sixth grade.

I like school and I have a lot of friends. Oh, I'm not the "queen of the class" or anything like that. That's not for me — all that showing off and acting conceited. I try to stay away from that kind of thing.

This year, in Kislev, a new girl named Nechama came into our class. The teacher gave her the seat next to mine. She looked like a really nice girl, but she was very shy — she didn't say a word.

Pretty soon, everyone realized that she was probably the smartest girl in the whole class. Her homework assignments were always beautifully done, and perfect. She never got less than ninety on a test. Little by little, she and I got acquainted. I say "acquainted" because although I would have loved to be her real friend, there was something about her that kept her from opening up and sharing herself with me.

I'll give you an example. After months of sitting right next to her, I still had no idea what her father did for a living, or whether she had any brothers and sisters, or even where she lived! In general, I always had the feeling that she was keeping some secret from me. And it was getting harder and harder talking to someone every day without knowing the first thing about her.

I decided to do something about it. One day, I offered to walk her home. But she tried to get out of it: "Oh, please don't to put yourself out," she said. "It's a very long walk."

We walked along together for quite a way, without speaking. I could see she wasn't comfortable at all. Then I saw she was turning toward the neighborhood near the railroad tracks — a poor, run-down neighborhood, with old, crumbling buildings. At the entrance to one of these, Nechama stopped. She said, "Thanks for walking me home," and disappeared very quickly into the building.

I stood there by myself, hurt and angry. Why couldn't she invite me up? This was my thanks for walking her such a long way? But, as quickly as it had come, my anger left me. After all, I realized, she hadn't been the least bit interested in my accompanying her. It was only my own curiosity that had dragged me here.

So I made up my mind that I wouldn't try to push my way into her life if she didn't want me to. We just continued the way we had been before. Gradually, though, we started becoming a little closer, and we spoke openly about lots of things, except... her family and her life. I discovered that she was a girl with a really good heart, that she was bright, gentle, and honest. I discovered many traits in her that I admired and that I wanted to learn, and I was just happy to be her friend.

One day I went into a nice clothing store near our school to look at a blouse I had seen in the window. I suddenly heard somebody say, "Nechama, did you choose one?" and then I heard a familiar voice answer, "Yes, I'm coming out." It was my friend's voice.

Without thinking too much, I decided to hide behind the rack. I peeked out and saw Nechama's mother, who didn't look at all like someone who lived near the railroad tracks. She was dressed in expensive clothing and looked very fancy. I heard her speaking to the manager too, and it sounded if she were a regular customer. The tone of voice he used was one of respect.

I decided to find out, once and for all. Once outside, I began to follow Nechama and her mother down the street, being very careful that they wouldn't see me if they turned around. They walked a few blocks and then entered the fanciest neighborhood in our city. It was an area with big private homes, each surrounded by a garden.

When I saw the two stop at a gate to one of these homes, I couldn't control myself anymore. "Nechama!" I called.

Nechama whirled around, saw me, and turned beet-red. Her eyes suddenly filled with tears.

Her mother didn't understand what was wrong. "Who is this, Nechama?" she asked. "A classmate?"

"It's Channy, the one I told you about," said Nechama, beginning to cry.

"So what's the matter?" her mother asked. But Nechama didn't answer.

After a moment's silence, her mother said, "Come in, girls, both of you, and we'll have a little talk." When we got inside, I started crying too, and I found myself telling her mother about our relationship, and about how much I wanted it to be a real friendship, but how Nechama wouldn't let it, because she insisted on hiding her life from me.

"All this time I thought Nechama was from a very poor family and that she was ashamed of it. But now that I see you're really not poor at all, I just don't understand…"

Nechama's mother was every bit as amazed as I. "Nechama, why didn't you want to tell Channy who you are and where you live?" she asked.

With a sigh, still crying a little, Nechama began to explain herself: "It's because of the way things were at the school I was in before we moved here. All the girls were rich, and they were all so conceited because of it. I hated the way they pranced around and boasted, and I could never get along with any of them because of it. When I came to your school, I made up my mind that no one would know my parents have a lot of money, so that they wouldn't think I was a snob." Nechama finished and took a few deep breaths.

We all sat and talked for a long time. Nechama's mother said she understood why she felt that way. But that the solution wasn't to close herself up like that and keep the truth about her life from all her new schoolmates. "You just have to work on being yourself, and people will appreciate you for what you are, not for how much money your parents have, or how nice your house is," she said.

"It's true, Nechama," I added. "We like you for yourself, and the other part doesn't matter."

We must have convinced her. The next day,

she really was a different person. She stopped hiding the truth about her family, and started inviting girls to her house. None of us felt any change in her character at all: Before she revealed her secret, she had been an easygoing, kind girl, and she was still exactly that. She was sincere and humble, and just "normal" and nice, and everyone loved her for it.

Is It Really
So Funny?

My name is Yehuda. I'm a really funny kid — everyone says so. I guess it's true.

From the beginning of first grade, I was always the class joker.

I know how to imitate people's voices, and all kinds of animal sounds. Everyone who hears me do it can't stop laughing.

I'm also good at telling jokes in a way that makes everyone laugh. For example: If I'm telling a joke about a chicken, I can twist my face and my body into the shape of a real chicken — including the beak! I mean, even someone who can't hear what I'm saying laughs at how well I do the impersonation.

I'll tell you the truth, though. Sometimes, I would like to be serious, but I think all the kids expect me to keep them laughing. I enjoy showing off, and being noticed, so I just tell another joke, and do another impersonation. As long as I keep their attention. That's the main thing. That's how I am....

Before Pesach this year, the teacher asked me to cite a *pasuk* that was connected to Pesach. I looked at him with a really straight face, and I said, "When Adar begins, joy increases." He raised his eyebrows and gave me a long, serious look. The whole class laughed, but even after they had quieted down, the teacher was still giving me that look. I really felt uncomfortable, as if he were looking straight into my *neshamah*!

After the class ended, the teacher asked me to stay behind in the classroom.

"Yehuda," the teacher began as soon as we were alone, "just try to picture what would have happened if, when Moshe *Rabbenu* informed *bnei Yisrael* that they were leaving Mitzrayim, there had been a comedian among them, someone who made a joke out of everything he said. What do you think? I'll tell you — we might still be in Mitzrayim today, *chas v'shalom*.

"You see, the whole reason why the People of Israel suffered and were afflicted for those forty long years in the wilderness was because of a small group of people. They were very bright people, but, in a way, they were clowns, because they made light of what was really important. And Korach was the same. Remember the saying that 'one joke can offset a hundred rebukes.'

"I don't mean for you to discard your talent completely. And it *is* a talent, a talent that Hashem gave you. But please try to think about how you can use it to bring *joy* to people, and not to mock things." The teacher finished his speech, gave me a pat on the back, and walked away.

I sat there for a while, lost in my thoughts. Memories flashed through my mind: how I had imitated Yossi, the most studious boy in the class — the way he holds his head between his hands, putting his fingers in his ears, to concentrate on his studying. How I made fun of an old lady who was crossing the street with a basket in each hand — a complete impersonation, down to the eyeglasses at the tip of my nose, as I waddled from side to side.

For some reason, none of it seemed funny anymore. I felt a bitter taste in my mouth, and tears forming in my eyes. "How could I do that?" I asked myself. "I don't have a cruel heart — I'm sure I don't."

"There's no question about it," I told myself. "The teacher is right. Laughter has tremendous power. It can change the way a person thinks. It

can wipe away, in an instant, the most important things there are. Making people laugh is a
power that has a dark and frightening side. But
on the other hand," I reassured myself, "it is
also possible to laugh and to make others laugh
without doing any damage." Then another idea
came to me. "In fact if I make fun of things that
are bad, I can help people and do something
useful."

Don't worry — I haven't changed into a kid
with no sense of humor. I'm still the class joker,
but somehow everyone has started taking me
more seriously now. You see, I myself have be-
gun to take things — if they're important things
— seriously.

The truth is, after all, that life is no joke.

Stay Away from Strangers

My name is Malky.

Until about half a year ago, I was one of the top kids in the class. My grades were high, and every time the teacher asked a question, I would raise my hand to answer. During recess, I ran around and played all the games, and lots of times, I was the winner. My parents were always very proud of me.

But half a year ago, all that changed.

Suddenly, I stopped paying attention in class. The teacher started telling me, again and again, to stop dreaming. During recess, I just sat in the classroom waiting for the bell to ring to bring the kids back.

Every morning, I told my mother I wanted to stay home with her instead of going to school.

Sometimes I even convinced her, and I missed a lot of school days.

This made my parents miserable, as you can imagine. All of a sudden, they saw their daughter change, become a different girl, and fall way down in her studies.

My mother tried to talk to me about it. She kept asking me: "Malky, what's happened to you? Is anything troubling you? Tell me!"

But I kept quiet.

One evening my parents came into my room and closed the door. They wanted to talk to me, they said. They knew that I was hiding something, and I even saw tears in my mother's eyes when she hugged me and said, "Tell us, Malky — whatever it is, we'll help you."

But I just looked at them, and didn't say a word.

I could not talk about the thing that happened, that made me change. I just was not able to say the words. Now I realize that I made a big mistake. How many days and months did I lose, hurting myself and others, just by holding the terrible and frightening secret inside.

My heart almost burst from guarding such a scary secret. After struggling really hard and long with it, I finally did tell the whole story to my mother one day. I left nothing out.

I'm not going to tell you everything, but I will

tell part of it, so that you'll know how to watch out, and so that you won't — God forbid — fall into the same trap as I did.

It happened on a Monday afternoon, six months ago. It's a day I will never forget as long as I live.

I was walking down the street, when a man I didn't recognize came over to me and said, "Hi, Malky — could you help me carry something upstairs?" I agreed.

I went with him, and what happened next is a secret that makes me cry every single time I remember it, even now.

My mother had always warned me not to talk to strangers, but I just couldn't imagine that this man would harm me. And he didn't *seem* like a stranger. He looked nice and kind, and reminded me of my father. I thought he was one of my father's friends.

To this day, I can't figure out how he knew my name. Maybe he saw it on my schoolbag. I think it was the fact that he called me by name that gave me the feeling that he knew me.

I am still suffering from that mistake.

When I finally did open up and talk to my mother, and then to my father too, I felt that a gigantic stone had fallen off my heart. My heart had been too small to carry around such a heavy, awful secret for so long.

My father talked to me about it for a long time. Then he took me with him to the police station. They were very nice, and a policewoman showed me lots of pictures of all kinds of criminals, so that they might be able to identify the bad man and keep him from walking around the streets waiting for other little kids.

My father also took me to a Rav, who spoke with me and made me feel better.

About a month later, the police really did catch the man. Boy, was I glad! Now I know that he won't be able to hurt anyone else.

I'm writing all this in order to warn you never to go off with someone you don't know, even if he tells you a convincing story. Remember that bad people can be good liars. Don't be afraid to say no to a grown-up.

The only people you have to listen to always are your mother and father, your grandparents, your big brothers and sisters, and your teachers.

I listened to my parents. I told them my secret, and then I was able to go back to being almost the same Malky as before. Almost.

My name is Asher.
My father says he's proudest of me
because I'm the best in Gemara and
the best in writing, and I hope I'll
stay this way. And I feel really
happy and lucky about this.

My name is Menachem.   ב״ה
I'm nine now but when I was seven our whole class
went to a big playground and I was on the seesaw
and fell hard onto an iron pipe and broke my
leg and my teacher ran over and picked me up
and took me to the hospital in his own car. We got
to the hospital and they put me on a stretcher
and they put a giant cast on me almost my whole
body was in it and everything hurt me so much and
I was so scared every time the doctor came in
cause every time he had to do something to me
it really hurt. After about a week they sent me home
from the hospital and all my friends came to see me
at home and they were all so jealous that I could stay
home from school for such a long time and I was so
jealous that they didn't hurt so much as me. After I was
in bed for a month and a half with that cast the doctor
said I could start to walk with crutches and I
walked with crutches for eight weeks.
And now I am all better, baruch Hashem.
                                                    Menachem.

A New Life

My name is Tomer. I'm the same age as the rest of you, and I live at the edge of Bnei Brak, not far from some of you. But my story is a very different one.

You boys always had *peyos*, and I never did. I never covered my head with a yarmulke. I come from a family that was called "secular."

I live in a neighborhood that's full of religious people. I never understood why they looked so different from me.

There's a boy named Yanki who lives next door to me. He's religious, and he has lots of friends who are always coming to play with him. They seem so nice, and I always wished they would include me in their games.

Once I actually went over to Yanki and I asked him quietly, "Why don't you ever invite me to join your games? And how come you never come over to my house, or invite me to yours?"

Yanki looked at me kindly, and he thought for a long time before he answered me. "Please understand," he began, "that I don't have anything against you, Tomer. It's just that our education is not at all like yours. There are things that you do that we are forbidden to do. Like on Shabbos, for instance. And there are things we do, and say, that you wouldn't understand. I'm not blaming you," he added quickly, to make me feel better. "But even though you are a very nice boy, it would be hard to be close friends — because, well, our ways of life are very different...."

I nodded. What he said made me feel terrible. I was really hurt. But I wasn't angry at him. And in a funny way I even understood him.

About two weeks later, I decided I couldn't take it any more. I had been studying up on religious people and their lives for some time, and I found myself feeling jealous of them. Take Shabbos, for example. They have a special Shabbos table with candles, and a pretty tablecloth. The whole family gets together and sits around the Shabbos table, all dressed up. The father is happy, and he smiles as he listens to the whole family singing Shabbos songs. (On Friday nights I can even hear the singing in my house!) Sometimes it's quiet, and — this is what some kids told me — that probably means one of the children is giving some explanations of

things that are written in the Torah.

All this looked so nice, and sounded so good to me. I found myself sitting near the window Friday nights, listening to the sounds coming from Yanki's Shabbos table. I even found tears rolling down my cheeks, I so much wished I could be part of that scene.

My house is so boring on Shabbos. My older brothers are always asking my father to give them money so they can go off somewhere. And I stay home. I don't have anything to do, and my parents are even busier than they are during the week and I'm really bored.

Meanwhile, Yanki's house seems so happy, so... *special.*

One day during the next week, after I had spent days arguing the thing back and forth in my mind, I made my decision. I went over to Yanki and I asked him, "Do you think you could bring me a yarmulke from your house?" He looked at me in amazement, but he quickly answered, "Yes, of course." He ran off, and within minutes there was a yarmulke on my head.

Then I asked, "Um... would you mind if I came to the *beit knesset* with you?"

"Why should I mind?" he answered, smiling. We both walked off to the *beit knesset.* It was five o'clock. A man was standing outside, calling "*Minchah, minchah!*" Yanki explained that this was the afternoon prayer, which had been established by Yitzchak *Avinu*. I happened to know who Yitzchak *Avinu* was — the son of Avraham *Avinu*. We had learned about all the Forefathers in school.

I read the prayer in the *siddur*, and I tried to imitate the movements Yanki made while he prayed. After we read a short prayer that started with "*Ashrei yoshvei beisecha*," there was *Kaddish*. Then Yanki whispered to me that everyone would be saying a longer prayer called *Shemoneh Esreh*, and that during that you're not allowed to move. I watched Yanki carefully. He put his feet close together, bent over for a minute, and started to pray. I did everything the same way.

I saw all the other kids watching me in amazement. I could imagine how surprised they were, and I was really grateful to them for not laughing out loud at my ignorance.

The prayer ended. I had enjoyed reading the words — more than anything I had ever read. The part I liked best was where it said, "You bestow knowledge upon man." It made me realize that now I have someone to ask when there are things I don't know or can't understand. And when I got to the part that asks God to "Cure us," I felt like crying because I thought of my dear Aunt Chemda who's in the hospital. I prayed to God that He would make her better.

I went home and told my father what I had just done. He listened to me with a strange look on his face and didn't say a word.

I started going to pray *minchah* and *ma'ariv* every day, and I began to get more and more familiar with the prayers. After a while, I didn't have to keep looking at Yanki.

One Friday afternoon, I asked my father if he would come with me that night to the *beit knesset*. Again, he looked at me with a strange, silent look. Then he shrugged, went into his room, and took a yarmulke out of his drawer. He held out his hand to me and said, "Come, Tomer," and off we went. When we were inside, I saw that my father was very moved by the praying. There were tears in his eyes.

On the way back, he didn't speak. When we got home, there was that boring quiet that I so hated. And then, all of a sudden, there was a knock on the door. It was Yanki!

"My parents would like to invite your whole family to come and join us for the Shabbos meal," he said.

My mother was embarrassed, and she hesitated. But my father said, "Thank you very much," and to my mother: "Come!"

We all went. My father and mother, my two brothers, my sister, and I. At the beginning,

we were a little tense and uncomfortable. But, little by little, we started humming along with the beautiful melodies Yanki's family sang. We listened very carefully to all the words of Torah, and I enjoyed every minute of it. I looked at my parents and at my brothers and my little sister and I saw that they were paying close attention to everything.

Can you believe that Shabbos meal ended at close to midnight! When we got home, none of us said a word, and none of us took off our yarmulkes.

The next morning, it was my father who woke up all his sons. "Come on, let's go to the *beit knesset*," he said. We all got up, and that's exactly where we went.

I won't make this story too long. My family is now becoming religious. I have switched to Yanki's school. My older brothers study Gemara privately with Yanki's father. He's a Rav and he's preparing them to enter a yeshiva.

It's not easy, this *teshuvah*. In school, everyone can tell I didn't have a religious upbringing. I don't act like the rest of the kids. But at least they understand, and most of them are polite and patient with me most of the time. They all try to explain things to me before I have to do them, so I won't be embarrassed. When I goof, they try to send me hints so no one else will see.

They give me more consideration, and they care more about how I feel, than any friends I ever had.

It's not easy, but it's all worth it when I sit down at our own Shabbos table. My mother has a scarf on her head, the Shabbos candles are lit, my brothers and I sing all the songs we have managed to learn, and we do our best to share words of Torah with each other.

How can I tell you what a wonderful feeling it is?!

Smartie

My name is Shmuel. Everyone calls me Shmulik. I'm, well, *really* smart. I heard my mother tell my father so — secretly, so that I wouldn't hear. They don't tell *me* because they don't want me to become stuck-up. But I know it, believe me. I know it very well.

Every morning, I pick up the newspaper and read about what's going on in the world. Then I go and ask my father tons of questions. Sometimes he enjoys my questions. Sometimes I surprise him, and he says that my questions are the kind grown-ups would ask. And sometimes, he doesn't even know how to answer me.

I love to show everyone how much I know. But my mother doesn't like it — she always tells me that it's not nice, that it's showing off. Actually, I don't know why I do it all the time. I guess I like it when people pay attention to me. I like people to smile at me, and to say I'm smart.

In class, I'm the top student. In tests, I get the highest marks. Each time the teacher asks a question, I raise my hand first with the answer. When other kids have trouble with schoolwork, I'm the one they come to, and I always help them.

Once, though, the teacher asked me if I help others because I like helping people, or because I want to show them how much I know. I turned red, and felt really uncomfortable. I don't like being asked questions like that.

Sometimes, deep down inside, I feel that the kids in my class don't like me all that much. I don't know why they shouldn't — I mean I *am* the smartest! Maybe they're just jealous.... but Avraham's also very smart, and nobody seems jealous of him. It seems they like him a lot. I wonder what the difference between us is.

Well, I know the difference, actually.

Maybe I should — sometimes — keep quiet in class, even when I do know the answer. Maybe I shouldn't show off so much? But it's so hard for me not to. I've tried.

And anyway, I think the rest of the kids look up to me, and wish they were as smart as I am.

But the truth is — I'm really kind of lonely.

The Quiet One

My name is Libby. I'm an ordinary girl, a little on the tall side, with brown eyes. Just a regular, ordinary girl.

I do have one problem, though: it's really hard for me to talk. I just keep my mouth shut, for no special reason, all the time. I sit in class and I never disrupt the lesson, but I never participate either.

Sometimes the teacher asks me a question, but I answer in such a soft voice that she has to keep repeating, "What? What did you say?" In the end, she always has to come and stand next to me and lean over to hear what my answer is. Or else, she calls me over to her desk and then I say — or rather, whisper — my answer into her ear.

Lately, she almost never asks me anything. It just takes too much of her time.

Sometimes, there'll be something I don't understand in class, but I don't ask. I'm too shy. My mother keeps telling me that my shyness is a serious problem. She quotes the Mishnah to me: "The bashful one does not learn." She tells me, "Just put all that shyness behind you, and ask!"

She's right.

But whenever I want to speak, the words just get stuck in my throat and refuse to come out, and I start to turn red, and to get embarrassed, and there's just no way....

I've tried to figure out why this happens to me. The only explanation I can find is one fuzzy memory that I recall when I think about the problem.

When I was in first grade, I answered some question that the teacher asked. I can't remember now whether I didn't know the answer at all, or whether the answer I gave was wrong. Whatever the case was, I just remember everyone in the class laughing at me. I was only six but I think maybe I decided then that if I didn't speak anymore, no one could laugh at me.

But now I'm ten and I guess that a "decision" like that was not too smart. I mean, I hardly have any friends. What are kids supposed to do with a girl who doesn't speak? I think I'd like having some friends, to tell you the truth, but my shyness ruins everything.

It happens sometimes that the teacher asks a question, and nobody knows the answer except me. But I won't raise my hand. I'm too shy.

My teacher is so good to me. She really tries to help me get over my shyness, but she can't manage to break through it. And neither can I.

Sometimes I think that — maybe — if some friends would just come over to me, start talking to me, invite me to play with them, and actually *make* me talk to them, it might do the trick. I wish somebody would tell them to do that. As for me, I'm too shy to tell them.

The teacher suggested to me that I try to speak loudly, and slowly, a little at a time. To try reading a small paragraph out loud, and then, little by little, to read longer ones. Just to get used to talking!

Maybe I'll try that. I don't know. Maybe.

My name is Miri. Till yesterday I thought the whole class hated me. About a month ago I had a fight with Yittie who sits in front of me, and Yittie told the teacher on me. The teacher said I should come to her at lunch period because she wanted to talk to me. I got real scared because I didn't know what the teacher wanted to talk to me about. The bell finally rang. I went into the teacher's room, and then the teacher came in. I was so scared. But the teacher started talking to me nicely. "Miri, what's been troubling you lately? How come you fight with the other girls?" I was afraid to tell her how I feel, so I just said I didn't know. Then she said "Maybe you're not sitting in a good seat. Which girl would you like to sit next to?" So I told her, "Near Dvorie, Baila, or Chana." The teacher sent me off to eat and when we came back into class, she changed my seat. After a few days, I had a fight with another kid. The teacher yelled at me, and I started to cry. She said, "Miri, I don't understand why you fight with all the girls." I answered her crying, "Because they all hate me." She said, "Oh! Now I understand. How do you know they hate you?" So I told her that every time I want to play on the swing, the girls playing there push me away. She said, "That doesn't mean they hate you, it just means there are usually other girls waiting their turn before you. That's all. They don't hate you. They like you!" Then she took a vote to see who likes me. Everybody in the class raised their hands. So during recess, the teacher gave me my punishment. She made me write, "Everybody likes me" fifty times. On the other side of the paper, she made every girl in the class sign her name. When I saw all the names, I felt better.

Redhead

My name is Noach. I'm in third grade. I'm cheerful and lively, and well, maybe a bit too lively....

Oh, I forgot to add something. I'm a redhead.

They say that redheads have a fiery nature, like their hair which resembles a burning fire. I agree with that. It sure is true of me. I always have something to do, and I do everything with lots of energy.

Until this year, I was the only redhead in the class. Then, at the beginning of the year, a new kid named Ronnie came into the class. When I first saw him, I was a little disappointed. Why? Because Ronnie was a redhead, just like me, and, well... Anyway, eventually I decided that if there could be ten kids in the class with brownish hair, ten with blondish hair, and ten more with black hair, I could handle it if there was one redhead in the class besides me....

And, right away, I saw that he was just exactly like me!

He knew how to handle a situation, how to talk, how to play — everything, just like me. But there was something different about him. A kind of sensitivity. He seemed to get all red and angry right away whenever some little thing happened. On the other hand, I did notice he liked to spend his time with me more than with anyone else.

And we really did become friends. Good friends. Once, when we were playing ball, Ronnie was out a few times in a row. Each time he was one of the first out. The fourth time it happened, he walked off the baseball field in a huff, yelling, "I know why... it's because I'm a redhead, that's why!"

I was really shocked. What on earth was he talking about? I asked him.

He turned to me and said, "Come on, now — haven't you noticed that you and I are different from all the others? Haven't you noticed that the two of us have... red hair?"

"Sure," I answered. "So what?"

"So *what?*" he retorted, surprised. "Everybody treats redheads differently from other kids — as if we redheads have a problem."

"Problem?" I really didn't understand him.

"Problem?" I asked again. "I think it's just the opposite. I'm really happy to be a redhead. Ever since I was little, I can remember my father saying, 'You're a carrot-top! You're a redhead like David *Ha-melech*!' with such joy on his face that I always knew it was something good. And I still feel that way. Why, 'red' was even my first word, and everyone in the family was thrilled. I've always been the special one in our family. How can you call it a *problem*?"

I was so excited that even my face was bright red by the time I finished making my speech (after all, I *am* a redhead).

Ronnie was looking at me in amazement. He just stood there for a while with his mouth open. Then he said, "I can't believe what you're saying. Everyone always treated *me* as if my red hair was a problem. I mean, it's true that I often got off the hook because of it. My parents would sometimes excuse my wild behavior because it must have come from being a redhead. As if redheads are just known to be hot-tempered. And if I get really mad or hit my sister or something, then they say it's my hair's 'fault!' So I always figured that having red hair was a problem. And now you come along and tell me it's something good. And it sounds from the way you talk as though you really are happy about being a redhead."

"Of course I'm happy," I cried out in a loud voice, "I'm a redhead! I'm a redhead!" By then I was shouting, and all the other kids had stopped playing to listen. They burst out laughing.

"You see?" I told Ronnie. "Just put that nonsense out of your head — out of your red head. Start being happy about your red hair, and you'll soon see that all your problems came from your own thinking that you had a problem, not from anyone else."

Since then, our friendship has grown even closer. Ronnie and I are the two best friends in the whole school. You can't keep us apart. Once we were walking together during recess and we heard a littler kid saying, "Those two redheads are something!" I looked sideways at my friend, and I saw him smiling happily. I didn't say anything, but in my heart there was a really good feeling.

The Artist

My name is Ruthie.

When I grow up, *b'ezras Hashem*, I'm going to be an artist!

Even now, I draw — all the time, and everything: my house, the neighborhood I live in, the view from my bedroom window, even the rays of sunlight that filter through the blinds.

After the rain you can find me sitting on the sidewalk drawing the puddles that are left. Drawing puddles may sound simple, but it's actually very complicated to capture the movements of the water. It's hard to put something like that into a drawing, because a drawing doesn't move.

I have a good imagination. But this very imagination that is so helpful to me when I draw actually makes problems for me in other areas.

For one thing, I'm lost in my thoughts almost

all the time, picturing things... in class, during recess, at home... My friends think I'm a little strange. They run around during recess, while I stare at the crooked fence beside the school-yard, trying to picture how I would draw it, how I would give it that look — as though it's about to fall over to the other side.

My mother appreciates my talent for draw-ing, and she's glad that I have it. But she tells me that even the greatest artist does not live in a dream world all the time, like I do. Sometimes when she asks me to wash the floor, I sit near the bucket of soapy water, studying the bubbles as they burst and disappear, drawing them in my mind... and then I remember what I'm supposed to be doing.

That may seem funny to you, but it makes my mother really, really angry. And she's right!

Once I drew a picture of how she looks when she's angry. I added creases to her forehead, and I emphasized her big, piercing eyes and the thin line of her mouth. I drew her eyebrows lowered, close to her eyes. I drew every single angry feature. And when my mother saw the picture, she was so surprised that she stopped being angry and started to laugh.

When people enjoy my drawings, I feel won-derful. It's like getting "Excellent" on a test. But I have to admit that I don't really know what it's like to get "Excellent" on a test. I've never received a grade like that (except in art class, of course).

There are a few other girls in my class who draw well, but they're not like me — they devote their time to schoolwork as well as to artwork. While the teacher is explaining something over and over again, I concentrate hard and really try... to figure out how I would draw the spider webs which hang so delicately from the top of the window to the curtain, and from the curtain to the wall.

Now, I know how to draw spider webs pretty well, but here, since the curtain sways in the breeze, the webs form a changing pattern that is not so simple to get down on paper.

Even when I really make up my mind to listen and pay close attention to the teacher's words, I end up in a dream. Like when she was teaching *parashas Shelach* and describing the way the *meraglim* spied out the Land. I suddenly found myself picturing the way I'd draw them making their way among sharp boulders in the darkness, being careful not to be seen by the Kena'anim. There in the corner of the picture, I'd... Suddenly, the bell rang! Recess. But I didn't go out. I just sat in my seat and spent the whole recess dreaming on....

One day the teacher caught me drawing a

picture of her. She took the drawing away, but she didn't rip it up — she just looked at it for a while and put it in her pocket. After class, she asked me to stay and talk with her.

"Ruthie," she said, "you draw beautifully, and I can see that you really have talent. You may be a well-known artist some day. But a Jewish girl has many tasks to fulfill in this world, and while using her special talents is one of them, it's not the *only* one. She must also use her mind and her energies to learn, and — even more important — to keep the Torah and the mitzvos.

"Tell me," the teacher went on, "at home do you also dream and draw more than you should, like you do in class, and not always fulfill your tasks properly?" I nodded. "Then your drawing is keeping you from honoring your parents the way you should, Ruthie. How will you build the kind of life you should be building if all you do is draw all the time?"

I didn't have an answer. Suddenly I burst into tears, crying so hard that I couldn't stop myself. The teacher hugged me and tried to calm me down. "I'm sorry my words upset you so much, Ruthie. But try to think about what I said." She said goodbye very warmly, and I went home.

All afternoon, I kept thinking about my teacher's words. I knew that what she had said was right. My drawing is a good thing, a positive thing, but it's certainly not the only thing in the world. I know Hashem wants more important things from me.

That night, I fell asleep and dreamed very strange dreams. My mother and my father on horse-drawn wagons, and my teacher....

I got up, turned on my light, and decided to try and draw the dream. Now that's a really hard thing to do, because a dream is so vague, and the images aren't clear. I decided to draw the whole thing inside a big cloud, to give the feeling of a dream. I put my father into one wagon with my mother. I put a crown on my father's head, because I love him so much. Then I started to draw my teacher.

Suddenly, I heard a rustling sound behind me. It was my father! He must have been standing there for some time.

My father had never really spoken to me before about my drawing, but his eyes always told me that he was unhappy about it being the only thing in my life. Now, he just turned silently and left the room.

I ran after him crying, and said: "Abba, I want to change. I want to do better in school, and to help Imma more, but I don't know what to do. I just love to draw so much!"

My father said, "Do you think we aren't proud

of your drawing, Ruthie? Your drawing is wonderful. But everything in this world has to have limits. Eating is important, for example, but if a person does nothing but eat all day, he'll grow impossibly fat. Any one thing that occupies all of a person's time keeps him from becoming a complete person.

"I very much want you to keep up your drawing," my father continued. "When you grow up, you'll have a profession you love to work in. But," he added, "you have to learn about all kinds of other things as well. You'll want to learn many things you'll need to know, especially how to educate your own children one day."

I sighed, and told him I just didn't know how to start. He gave me a suggestion. "Try to pay attention to what the teacher is saying for fifteen minutes. Just work on that — fifteen minutes of listening to her and thinking only about what she is teaching. When you find that you can do that, add five minutes more of concentration. I think that, little by little, you will learn to keep your daydreaming under control."

I decided that I would try hard to do what he said. And it's working!

Now everyone can tell that something about me has changed. I listen better and I participate in the lessons. During recess I run around and play with my friends. No, of course I haven't stopped drawing, but the important thing is that I have really started studying in school, and helping my mother in the house, like a normal girl!

Yesterday, when my teacher came into the classroom and opened her roll book, she found a colorful drawing tucked into it. It showed a girl holding a broom in one hand and a schoolbook in the other. Behind her on the wall were a lot of paintings and sketches. She looked up and found my eyes, and gave me a long hard look, and then a big smile to show that she understood what I was trying to tell her.

What Is Strength?

My name is Danny. I'm in fourth grade.

I am not a healthy boy. I was born with a disease that affects my growth and the way I move. I have a lot of problems with my body. I can't eat and drink the things other kids can, and it's hard for me to walk. I do everything very slowly. Most of the things you kids can do without even thinking, are very hard for me.

When I began to realize how different I was from other kids, I was angry all the time. Why couldn't I be like everyone else? But, after a while, my parents helped me to see that Hashem has His own reasons for doing things the way He does, and I learned to accept my situation.

The truth is, I have so many things to thank Hashem for! The main thing is that my mind is not affected by the disease. *Baruch Hashem*, I understand everything they teach in school and I can answer the questions the teachers ask. It's true that it's very hard for me to write. I told you I was slow, right? But I sit during recess, and then for hours after school, and — very slowly — I write letter after letter after letter until I have written everything I need in my notebook.

The teacher always tells me that I don't have to write everything. But I want to prove to him, and also to myself, that I can do it.

Sometimes I see kids who don't do all their homework, and I really can't understand it. I'm so grateful to Hashem that I can know the answers and that, even if it takes lots of hard work, I can write them all. And they — the kids who can write all of it so quickly and easily — they just throw away such a big present from Hashem!

Because of my problem, I'm allowed to leave the room whenever I want. I heard the principal tell my teacher at the beginning of the year, "Danny has a special problem. Let him leave the room any time he wants to." And I thought, Wow! I'm so lucky, I can just go out any time! But then I realized that I'd only be hurting myself by missing things the teacher said, for no reason. So now I go out only when I really have to.

I think that kids don't thank Hashem enough for making them healthy. If they only knew how hard it is for me to use my body, I bet they'd start using their bodies only for good things.

Speaking of other kids, I want to tell you about the kids in my class. They are so wonderful. They treat me so nicely. They help me whenever they can, and they make me feel like I'm just like any one of them. None of them ever made fun of me or made me feel bad. Just the opposite — if I'm going somewhere with my friends, and any other kid on the street laughs, my friends make sure that kid apologizes to me. They are really amazing, my friends.

One day, I went out of class with another boy, Levi, to take a drink. On the way back, I stopped halfway down the hall, and I asked him to race me back to the class.

He said, "Sure," and we counted to three and started running. We both ran and Levi got there three seconds after me. "I won!" I cried out, thrilled. And Levi said, "Yes, you did." I told all the kids in the class that I had won the race, and Levi just nodded.

Now, you have to understand that when I run with every ounce of my strength, it's like any one of you walking slowly. So, after the joy of my victory wore off, I realized that Levi could run a whole lot faster than me any day. But he made sure to go very slowly so that I could win. I was so touched when I thought about it, because I know that no kid ever likes to be the loser, but here Levi lost on purpose so that I could have the good feeling of being a winner for once.

At recess, I went over and just hugged him. He acted like he didn't know why, but he clapped me on the shoulder in a friendly way and smiled.

I just wish all the kids in the world knew how to be real friends like the kids in my class.

Best Girl
in the Class

I'm not going to tell you who I am, because I don't want other kids to think I'm bragging. You'll see what I mean in a minute.

I'm considered the best student in my class. I pay attention in all the lessons, I participate in every discussion, and I raise my hand to answer all the questions. I don't remember ever giving the wrong answer!

I'm the first to finish a test, and I always get "Excellent." If any girl in the class has a question about homework, she can always come to me for the answer.

Also, they say that my handwriting is the neatest in the class — so at the beginning of every school year, my teacher from the year before asks me for my notebooks. It makes me feel really good, but you know, there are girls who are a little bit jealous of me. I sometimes overhear kids whispering about me, and saying something like, "What's the big deal? She's smart, she knows it all, so it's no problem for her to be the best in the class!"

Do they think some angel comes and brings me knowledge while I sleep, and that I don't have to work at it?

Let me tell you: it's not what they think — not at all. The fact is that I live with a lot of tension, and even real fear. I simply cannot let myself go into class without being perfectly prepared. I'm afraid that the teacher will call on me and I won't know the answer. Everyone is so used to me knowing, that I'm sure they'd all giggle and talk about me if once I didn't know an answer. And that makes me feel afraid. The secret of all my knowledge is a simple one: I spend a tremendous amount of time on my homework every night. I know for sure that there are girls in the class who are smarter than I am — but they don't put as much time and energy into being "number one."

Sometimes the work is hard for me, and there are really things I don't understand. So I sit and go over them again and again until really late at night. My father says it's great to be studious, and that having patience to sit and learn is a wonderful quality. But it's just a shame, he says, that my studiousness comes from fear of failure. "We'd be happy if you came home with an 80 or even a 70 on a test sometimes," my parents tell me. "We'd love you and be every bit as proud of you if you were number two or three in the class!"

But it doesn't help — I can't stop being afraid.

Believe me, it is not easy being the best in the class!

The teacher relies on me, and she sends me on responsible errands. My parents do too, and I feel good about being taken seriously. And don't think that I'm such a serious girl that I never smile, or anything. No — you can see me doubled over with laughter sometimes. And I run and dance, and jump rope like any other girl. I know kids have to play sometimes — we're not grown-ups. But in order to succeed in life, I think you really do have to be serious and think about things before you do them.

Anyway, I've told you a little about my life and I hope I made myself clear to you. Maybe now you understand a bit more about what goes into being "the best girl in the class."

My name is Naomi.
When my brother got a hit in his eye we checked the mezuzah in his room and the word einecha was pasul.

My name is Daniel.
My family is not so happy. I have a big brother in yeshivah, and after him, I was born, and after me I have a little sister. She's not an ordinary girl — she's handicapped. After her, I have a younger brother. I'm not going to tell about everybody in my family separately, just my little sister. Her legs are paralyzed, and she doesn't know how to talk, and she can't even get around in a wheel chair. So, with Hashem's help, we're moving to a bigger apartment. But don't think it's fun. It's very hard to leave all my friends. We're not moving because of us, we're only moving because of her. I really really hope that she'll walk, or even that she'll get around in a wheelchair, with Hashem's help.

A Day of
Songs and Smiles

My name is Ephraim. I'm in fifth grade. I'm pretty good at schoolwork. I'm a short kid, but it doesn't disturb my life one bit. My mother likes to say that what a person lacks in height, he can make up for in brains. And I can see that she's right. The fact is that even though I'm the shortest in the class, I'm head of the class council and I've organized the school choir.

One day, the teacher gave me a message: "The principal would like to see you, Ephraim."

I got scared. What could I have done? The whole class looked at me with pity, and I walked really slowly to the principal's office, trying to figure out what I might have done wrong to deserve a punishment or a scolding.

But the principal didn't look at all angry.

Smiling, he offered me a chair across the desk from him, and he said: "There's something I want to ask you, Ephraim. I just got a call from an old-age home which is nearby. They asked if I could send them a group of boys next week, to sing for the old people for Chanukah and make them happy."

I felt like a stone had fallen off my heart, and I sighed with relief. The principal smiled again. He must have known what I had been thinking. Then he said, "Think you can do it?"

"Sure," I answered eagerly, and I gave him a list of the kids I thought would be good for this project.

But then, when I went to tell the boys about where we would be going, they weren't very enthusiastic at all. "How boring! What fun could we have in an old-age home?" they said, but they finally agreed to go.

And then I started to wonder myself. How would this work? How would the old people receive us? Would we really be able to make them happy? Would they cooperate with us? Even though I was nervous about it, I tried to get the other guys excited. We decided which songs we would sing and then rehearsed a bit.

The big day finally came and a taxi arrived at school to take us to the old-age home.

When we got to the main room, all the old people were sitting in their chairs waiting for us. Some of them were talking to each other; others were just staring into space, not paying any attention to us at all. I saw that my friends were discouraged by the sight that greeted them, and I wasn't very hopeful either.

But an idea came to me, and I took matters into my own hands. I grabbed the mike and I said, loudly and enthusiastically, "Good afternoon to you all. Please pretend we're your grandchildren, and sing along with us." Then the band burst into Chanukah music, and we began to sing.

All of a sudden, the whole atmosphere changed. How can I describe what happened?

The old people came alive. They started clapping a little, and then they clapped louder and louder. Many of them were swaying to the music or tapping their feet to the beat. At first a few of them sang along with us, and then more joined in. And then, to our amazement, some of them got up and began to dance in place. Everybody seemed to be smiling. It was beautiful! I don't think I ever saw a whole roomful of people so happy.

Then, out of the corner of my eye, I noticed a woman whose eyes were only half open, who seemed completely indifferent to what was going

on. I thought she might be asleep, but then I saw her eyes moving, and I knew she was awake and, in fact, even paying attention to us.

I decided we should all sing louder, and I signalled the others. I moved a little closer to this lady, and sang straight at her. Sure enough, she perked up, and started tapping her hand lightly on the arm of her chair. She even smiled a little.

I knew I had done a mitzvah.

After the performance, the manager of the old-age home came over to us and said that in all the years since the place had first opened, he hadn't seen such a *simchah* there. "Some of these people haven't even spoken in months, and today they were laughing and singing!" he told us.

Well, on our way back, the other kids had to admit that I had been right. It sure was worth it. "I've never had so much fun," said one of the boys. We started to talk about how old people really are interesting, and how most younger people never even bother to try to talk to them or to reach out to them at all. If you only know how to act towards them, you find out that they can sing and be happy just like anyone else.

We wished there were somebody to make them happy all the time. Then we started thinking about how we might go there more often....

That night, while trying to fall asleep, I found

myself remembering that one old woman who hadn't been reacting to us at all until we succeeded in catching her attention. That moment stuck in my mind as the high point of the whole wonderful day.

I realized that the main thing for me had been more than just the discovery that old people are really people too. It had been learning that, with effort, you can bring a little happiness to someone who isn't able to make himself happy. That bit of joy on her face was the last thing I saw before falling asleep.

Henny's World

My name is Henny, and I'm in third grade.

I'm a little short and kind of small, but I'm good at my studies. I'm the oldest child in the family. I have three younger brothers and a baby sister.

In class, I'm considered quiet. I never make any trouble, and I'm not one of the first to answer. But I'm not one of those always-silent types, either. I just tend to be quiet by nature, that's all.

I always read in children's magazines, and in books like this, about the problems that kids have. I enjoy the stories — they're really interesting. But there's one thing I can't understand. Everybody seems to have some problem! I would also like to write about a problem, so I keep trying to think of one, but I can't.

You see, I don't *have* a problem. What can I do? I'm not troubled, and I'm not angry. I'm not painfully shy, and I don't hit other kids.

Life is good to me, nobody bothers me, I don't hate anybody, and I don't think anybody hates me.

I asked my mother what she thought about the problem of not having any problem. She gave me a big hug, and she laughed. "You're a very smart girl, Henny," she said. "You raise a very important question. Let me think about it."

That night at bedtime, my mother sat down on my bed, and she started to talk to me about problems. "You know," she began, "that although there are many problems in the world, many of the problems people have exist only because the person *thinks* he has a problem."

I opened my eyes wide. "I don't understand!"

My mother went on to explain: "Let me give you an example. Let's say there's a girl who's quiet by nature. She could look around at the lively girls in her class and think she's the most unlucky person in the world, just because she isn't like them. You, however, are quieter than most of your class, and yet you don't see this as a problem. And the truth is, it's not a problem. The world is full of quiet people who are very successful in every way."

I nodded. "Give me another example, Imma," I asked.

My mother thought for a moment and then

she said, "There are short children who feel that having less height makes them *less good*, less worthy, than other children. They spend all their time feeling sorry for themselves and being ashamed of their size."

"But, Imma," I said, "*I'm* short. And it doesn't bother me!"

"That's exactly what I mean, Henny dear," said my mother. "The only problem those others have is that they *think* they have a problem. If they accepted whatever Hashem gave them naturally, they wouldn't think of being ashamed of it — and they wouldn't have any problem at all!"

I thought about it for a minute. She was right. If I *wanted* to look for problems, I'd be able to find some. Take my little brother for example, who's always messing up my stuff and bothering me. My parents always tell me to be nice and patient with him because he's little. Now, I know kids who could make that into a real problem. But I know that it's no big deal — I'm older, so I have to be nice, and that's all there is to it.

I thought some more, with my mother smiling at me. "Give me another example," I asked her. She thought for a long time and then she found an example: "There are some children who get insulted very easily. They can take offense at almost anything another child says, even when the other one had no bad intention at all. Those children are creating a problem themselves where none exists."

It's true, I thought, as my eyes started closing. There's that girl in eighth grade who calls me "Henny-Penny" every time she sees me. I could get insulted, but instead I laugh and wave at her, happy that she notices me.

I guess Hashem gave me a special gift: that of not making problems out of nothing.

"Another example," I whispered to my mother, but I was falling asleep by then. I saw that I'd have to look for other examples in dreamland....

Special

My name is Naftali.

You know me. I always walk past your school. I don't go in — I just walk by. I don't go to your school, you see because I can't go to any regular school.

My school is different. It has a really nice name, and after the name they always say, "a school for special children."

Once I asked my mother, "What does 'special' mean?"

She was confused, and she asked me why I wanted to know. I told her why, so she sat down and started explaining a lot of things. I didn't understand most of it, but I could tell that "special" means different from other children.

I knew that before, though. I don't know if I knew for sure, but I always *felt* that I wasn't like most other kids in the neighborhood.

I think you also know that I'm different from

the rest of you. Maybe that's why so many children laugh at me and call me names. I always try to be so nice to other kids, to be friends. But most kids run away from me.

I'm used to it. To being "special," I mean. My mother explained that Hashem has His own plan for all of us. Everyone has good points, and everyone has bad points, and everyone has tests in life. This is my test. It's okay. I can handle it.

But there's one thing I can't get used to. I'll never get used to it. It's kids laughing at me. Why do they laugh? Are they mean? Maybe the bad point Hashem gave *them* is that they have no heart. I don't understand how they could laugh at somebody because Hashem decided to make him less smart. How could they laugh at somebody when they know it makes him cry?

I may not be so smart, and my brain may be different from yours, but my heart is exactly the same. I want the same things as you do. I want to have real friends. I want people to be nice to me.

Believe me, I never did anything bad to anyone. I never even hurt a bug. Why should I? It feels good to know that I never hurt anybody else. So, why am I so sad then? Why am I sitting here and crying?

Thank God, I do have one very good friend from your school. When I go past, he always stops to talk to me, and he acts as if I was just a regular kid.

I don't want to tell you who this boy is, because he's so dear to me. I want to keep him a secret. And I wouldn't want anyone to laugh at *him* for being nice to me.

The Mysterious Find

My name is Baila. I'm just an ordinary girl in fourth grade.

I have a long story to tell you. It took a whole year for all of it to happen.

One day — that's how stories start, right? — I was walking home from school when I saw a black case, lying right on the sidewalk. I picked it up and opened it, and discovered a camera inside. It had different lenses and dials, and it looked really complicated. I figured it must be very valuable.

I got home and showed my find to my mother. She helped me look all over the camera, inside the case and out, but there was no name — nothing at all to identify the owner. I took the camera to my room and turned it over and over in my hands. Suddenly, I had an idea. I ran back to my mother and cried, "Imma, there *is* a way to identify the owner! You said there's a roll of film in the camera, right? Then let's have it developed and the pictures will give us the clues we need to find out who owns it."

My mother agreed that it was a good idea, and off I ran to the photography store. I gave in the film, and waited impatiently for the pictures to be ready. An hour later, the man behind the counter told me sadly that of all the pictures, only one had come out. He showed it to me. What a strange picture! There was a gigantic frog in it, an Arab, a really weird-looking man in a striped uniform who looked as if he had just escaped from prison, a cute baby, and two men — one dressed like a Chasid, and another wearing a suit and hat.

I didn't recognize either man, and I thought the whole picture was the strangest I had ever seen. Wouldn't you? I just kept staring at it — right-side up, upside down — and the longer I looked, the more peculiar it seemed. Finally, the man at the counter said impatiently, "Young lady, you haven't paid yet and we're about to close." I quickly paid him for the developing, and ran home.

At home, I took out my magnifying glass, and went over every inch of the photograph. At the edge of the picture, I saw a table piled high with platters of cake and bottles of wine. This must have been some kind of *simchah*, I

thought. A careful look at the "prisoner" showed him to be less frightening than I had thought at first. It seemed he was a boy who had drawn a mustache on his face, and put on striped pajamas. And the frog didn't look too convincing either, I thought, realizing suddenly that it must be a frog *costume*. That Arab wearing a *keffiyeh* also seemed to be a kid....

Aha!

The picture must have been taken on Purim, when all the kids were dressed up — one as a frog, another as a prisoner, and a third as an Arab. I wasn't sure about the Chasid, though. The other man and the baby left no doubt in my mind — they were for real.

Well, I had solved the mystery of the weird snapshot. But the main mystery was still un-solved: Who were these people?

The ones in costume — forget it, I told my-self. How could I figure out who they were? And I didn't recognize the others at all. I asked my parents to help, but the people didn't look familiar to them. They were really impressed with my detective work, though.

My mother told me I should put up notices all around the spot where I had found the camera. She also encouraged me to call an ad in to the lost-and-found section of the newspaper.

We did all of those things. But no one called.

Many days, and then weeks, passed. The camera stayed on my shelf, and no one touched it, but I never forgot about it, or about the mitzvah of returning a lost object.

Sometimes, I'd just sit and stare at the picture and try to think how I could get to those people who had been photographed. Finally, I thought of something. These people, like all people, surely had dozens of relatives and friends, and hundreds of acquaintances. I decided to carry the picture around with me, and to show it to everyone I knew. Surely I'd find someone I knew who also knew one of the men in the picture.

Well, none of my relatives knew them, and neither did any of the girls in my class. For months, I showed that picture to everyone I met. Every visitor that came to us, everyone whom we visited, every *bachur* from the yeshivah next door, the bookseller and the grocer and the clerk in the post office... Unfortunately, all of them told me that they didn't know the people in the picture. While they were at it, they had lots of fun making cracks about the picture. ("Sorry, don't know any frogs." Or, "None of my friends are in prison." Or, pointing to the Arab, "I wouldn't *want* to know *him!*")

In spite of all of this, though, I never gave up.

One day there was a knock at the door. A

young man asked if we knew where the Rabinowitzes lived. We directed him to the building next door, without paying too much attention to him. When he started to leave, I jumped up, remembering. "Excuse me, could you wait just a minute?" I asked him. He turned and nodded, puzzled. I ran to bring him my famous photograph. "Do you know any of the people in this picture?" I asked him.

The young man stared thoughtfully at the picture. I couldn't believe my ears when he said, "Yes, I do. The Chasid in the picture is Rabbi Moses. He was my brother's teacher in yeshivah." I asked him if he knew where the rabbi lived, and he told me. My hands were actually shaking as I wrote down the address. When my mother came home and I told her, she found the phone number, and called the Moses home.

"Hello," said my mother. "Is this the Moses family?"

"Yes," answered a woman's voice.

"Did you by any chance lose a camera?"

"No, we didn't," the woman replied.

My mother apologized and hung up. "Sorry," she said to me, shrugging her shoulders.

"But it can't be!" I said. "That *bachur* said he's sure the man in the picture is Rabbi Moses."

Well, I decided that I would go over my-self and visit the Moses family. It took about twenty minutes to find the address. Hesitantly, I knocked on the door. A woman opened it, probably the same one who had answered the phone.

"Yes, dear, may I help you?" she asked me.

"I... I mean, the phone... my mother just called you about a camera!" I blurted out.

"Ah, yes, but we haven't lost a camera," said the woman. "I told your mother that."

"But still, I want to ask you to look at this picture," I said, "and see if you know the people in it." I held out the photograph.

She took it from my hand, and after study-ing it for a moment, she said, "Yes, this is my husband, and the 'Arab' is my son dressed up for Purim! I'm sure my husband would know who the others are. He should be home in about fifteen minutes. Would you like to come in and wait for him?"

I followed her inside and told her the story of finding the camera. She smiled at me and asked me to sit down. I waited impatiently. In ten minutes, the man from the picture suddenly appeared, in real life, right before my eyes. (His *shtreimel* was missing, of course, because this was just an ordinary weekday.)

His wife briefly told him the story and showed him the picture. "Do you know the other people in this picture?"

He put on a pair of glasses, and I felt like a coiled spring as I watched him study it. "Yes," he said, "that's Yossi's teacher, Rabbi Landman. We went to him on Purim to bring him *mishloach manos*, remember?"

The woman smiled at me brightly and said, "Now just wait a minute." She picked up a small phone book, flipped to the right page, and dialed a number. Here's what I heard then:

"Mrs. Landman? This is Esther Moses speaking. Is your husband at home? ... Oh. Well, can you tell me, then — have you lost a camera lately? ... *Yes*? Right after Purim? Well, there's a young lady here who found it!"

She called me over to the phone, but I was too shy to talk.

The next day, I brought the camera over to the Moses home. Their son, Yossi Moses, brought it straight to the Landmans.

That evening, I got a phone call. In a very emotional voice, Rabbi Landman thanked me for all my efforts to find the owner of the camera. "It's true that the camera is worth a lot of money," he said, "but the work you did and your strong desire to do the mitzvah of returning a lost object are worth far more to me. They are more precious than gold. You cannot imagine what a wonderful reward you will get from Heaven for working on this mitzvah for a whole year."

After thanking me again, Rabbi Landman hung up. Only then did I really feel the tremendous joy that comes from doing a mitzvah that involves so much work. Believe me, there's no feeling like it in the whole world.

Happy with My Lot

My name is Avi. And I'm fat.

When I was in kindergarten, all the boys used to call me "fatso" and I always felt terrible.

Then in elementary school they kind of stopped the name-calling, but any time anyone had a reason to insult me, there it was again. "You fatso!" And I — well, I had nothing to say. I *am* a fatso.

I've tried to lose weight. Many times. I mean, sometimes I've even almost starved myself for days. But it's so hard, and in the end, I always just stay fat.

The years go by, and my friends are used to me by now. I don't even think they particularly think of me as a "fatso" any more. At least they never act as though they do. But every time I look in the mirror, I can see that nothing has changed. I'm still fat.

I'm a fairly good student. Not the best in the

class, but good. And — something interesting — I don't really know why, but the other guys like me. I'm big — not just fat — and maybe I seem older to them, sort of. Anyway, I've heard them saying that I'm a good guy. And I think I am.

I don't dislike anyone. Not at all. I actually feel that all the guys are my friends. They come and tell me their secrets, and if any one of them has a problem, he tells me about it and I try to help him if I can.

It sounds funny, but I sometimes think my being fat comes in handy. Once, we were on a class trip and in this park a group of older kids came over to our class and started bullying the boys. So they called, "Avi! Avi!" When those older kids saw me coming, they turned around and ran away!

My house is always full of friends. I'm a happy kid, I like to laugh, and I like to make my friends laugh. And if anybody ever tries to make fun of me a little because of my weight, you know what I do? I say something even funnier about being fat, and turn the tables on the other guy. Once the others realize that I'm not insulted by that kind of talk, they stop teasing me.

But the truth is, it does bother me a bit. I'd love to be thin like some of the other kids, and be able to run around and do all the other stuff

they do. Still, I know this is not such a terrible problem. I mean, everyone has problems, and I'm not so sure I would want to swap mine for someone else's. I just hope I never have any worse problem than this.

And, in the meantime, I'm happy with my lot.

My Mother and Teacher

My name is Elisheva. I just started fifth grade.

On the first day of school, I felt excited and happy to be back. The classroom was freshly painted and beautifully decorated. All the girls were talking about the great things they had done during summer vacation. Then the topic switched to trying to guess who would be our homeroom teacher. It was lots of fun.

My good feeling lasted right up to the second the new teacher walked into the room. When she came in, my heart sank. I started feeling really uncomfortable.

Don't think I don't like this teacher. It's not that at all. Just the opposite. I love her, more than anyone else in the world. In fact, she lives in our house! We eat supper together every night, and...

Okay, that's enough! I'll explain: The new homeroom teacher is my mother.

Yes, my mother has been teaching in our school for fifteen years, and now she was assigned to teach the class that has her own daughter in it. But she hadn't said a word to me about it. She just walked into the classroom and surprised me. She explained to me later that she did it that way for my sake: she knew that if she'd told me before, I'd have worried about it endlessly (and she's right!).

Now, it's not easy to be in a class whose teacher is your own mother.

First of all, you have to behave yourself all the time. Imagine sitting in class with your mother right there in front of you, and you have an urge to play some practical joke, or to giggle. Several times, my mother caught me whispering to my neighbor, and she really let me have it. I was twice as embarrassed as I would have been if any other teacher had yelled at me.

And then, there's a problem with the other girls. Any time my mother lets me be the one to erase the board, say, or do any other job, there'll always be someone in the class to say she's playing favorites. I don't think the rest of them understand that I am under twice as much pressure as they are. They have a teacher in school to worry about. I have a teacher *and* a mother.

I was so uncomfortable with all this that I

couldn't get into my studies at all for the first few weeks of school. And the teacher — er, my mother, that is — would get really mad at me. After a while, though, I began to get used to the situation, and the other kids stopped whispering among themselves every time my mother made any comment to me.

Some things that happened were really funny, though. Once, before we went on a class trip, the teacher announced that we needed our parents' consent. She turned to me and said, "Elisheva, if you have any trouble convincing your mother to let you go on this trip, please tell me, and I'll have a word with her..." The whole class laughed. Even me.

But there were other things that weren't funny at all — in fact they were pretty strange. Once, I hadn't done my homework, and my mother gave me the usual "teacher's note" that she gives in such situations. The note read, "You should know that Elisheva has not done her homework. In the future, please see that she prepares each day's assignment." I looked at her, and tried to catch her eye to exchange a mother-daughter look. But — nothing. She kept her distance, acting like a stranger, like any teacher to a student who had misbehaved. I can't tell you what a horrible feeling that was.

That evening, I went over to her with the

note and said, "Imma, my teacher sent you this note." At first she remained very serious, but then she smiled and softened, and said to me, "I know you were surprised to see me treat you like someone else's child today. But you must understand, Elisheva, that even though I am your mother, I have to keep a certain distance as your teacher, and not just give you a smile that will excuse everything. Believe me, it was difficult for me — in fact, it is just as hard for me as it is for you to separate the fact that I am your mother from my classroom relationship with you. But I want my child — my student — to get the best possible education in every way, and this is part of what is necessary in order for that to happen."

Then, like a mommy and not like a teacher, she signed my note, scolded me, and asked me to promise that it wouldn't happen again. I promised.

All in all, you have no reason to envy me. It's no simple thing to be a student of your mother's. It's interesting, though. Very interesting.

Kindergarten Memories

My name is Yechiel. I'm in fourth grade now. I'm a good student. I don't disturb the class, but I'm not too quiet either. I'll tell you something, though — I am really *mad* at my kindergarten teacher.

I know you're probably wondering why on earth a big boy in fourth grade would be angry with a kindergarten teacher who hasn't taught him in four years.

Well, here's the story:

In the kindergarten in our school, like in many others, I guess, there are all kinds of games and toys. There's Lego, and blocks, and musical instruments and doctor kits.... At play time, every kid would pick what he liked, and he'd play with it. It usually worked out fine, except for one thing.

There was one toy that *all* the kids always wanted to play with. It was a kind of game set up on a gigantic wooden board. Roads had been drawn on the board, and little traffic lights stood at the corners. There were houses, trees, cars, and buses. There was a hospital, a police station, and wooden people. It was exactly like a real city. There were ten little cars that you could move yourself, anywhere along the roads. Every one of us loved that game the best. But only a few children could play at that board at one time, so the teacher would choose five boys each day, and call them by name.

She never once called my name!

A whole year passed, and not once did I get to go over to that board. When she'd choose the boys every morning, I always yelled the loudest that I wanted to play that game. Her eyes would go over the whole class, and she'd call a name, and then another, and another. Never mine.

I was so disappointed! I would find myself a corner, take one of the other toys to play with, and pretend to be playing. But I was in no mood to play. I was mad. Why didn't she like me? How could it be that I was the only one that never got picked? Now I wonder sometimes whether it was because I was always in the middle — not one of the best kids, not one of the worst kids. She just probably never noticed me. Boy, was I angry at her. It was so unfair!

It was a long time ago, true — but you

know what? Yesterday, I waited for school to end. When all the kids had gone home, I quietly went downstairs, and... I walked into the kindergarten room.

It was dark, but I knew where that board was set up. It was still standing in exactly the same place. I picked up one of the cars, and I started moving it around on the roads, up the hills, down into the valleys, among the trees, and right up close to the sidewalks. Just the way I'd always dreamed of doing!

It's true I've grown up since kindergarten days, and I know it's just a kiddie game and everything, but I don't think I ever enjoyed playing any game the way I enjoyed those few minutes.

Suddenly I felt a hand on my shoulder. I jumped. The principal had been going through the empty rooms to check before locking up, and had found me!

"Yechiel, why haven't you gone home?" he asked me softly. So I told him. I told him the whole, long story from the beginning. The story I just told you. I talked and talked, for I don't know how long. When I was finished, I just stood there quietly. The principal also stood quietly, looking at me.

After a few silent moments like that, the principal spoke quietly, like he always does: "You're right, Yechiel. It really was unfair, and it must

have hurt. The teacher was wrong. But you were also wrong. And I'll tell you why.

"If something is bothering a child," the principal went on, "he should speak about it. If you had gone over to that teacher and said, 'I've never once played with that game,' wouldn't she have let you play, right there on the spot?"

I nodded. "Yes, she would have."

The principal continued, "You have to understand, Yechiel, that we're all human. Everybody makes mistakes, even teachers. To hold so much anger and sadness inside you for four long years, when you could have prevented it all with a word to the teacher — what a shame!

"Go home now, Yechiel," he added gently, "and push all those sad and angry thoughts out of your mind. And anyway," he ended, "you did get to play with the game in the end, right?"

On the way home, I realized that my heart felt lighter. All the pain had disappeared, and the problem seemed to be such a little one. What was it, anyway? One more game, that's all.

I made a decision. Never again would I hold on to such things in my heart. I mean, a heart is not a storeroom.

Glossary

The following glossary provides a partial explanation of some of the Hebrew, Yiddish (Y.) and Aramaic (A.) words and phrases used in this book. The spellings and explanations reflect the way the specific word is used here. Often, there are alternate spellings and meanings for the words.

ABBA: father; Daddy.

AVINU: "our father."

BACHUR: a young man; a yeshiva student.

BAR MITZVAH: a Jewish boy of 13, the age at which he accepts religious obligations; the celebration marking the occasion.

BARUCH HASHEM: "Thank God!"

BEIT KNESSET: a synagogue.

B'EZRAS HASHEM: "With God's help."

BNEI YISRAEL: the Children of Israel; the Jewish People.

CHAVRUSA: (A.) a study partner.

CHUMASH: (one of) the Five Books of the Bible.

DAN L'CHAF ZECHUS: to judge others favorably.

DERASHAH: a sermon.

EINECHA: "your eyes."

IMMA: mother; Mommy.

KADDISH: a song of praise to God, recited as a mourner's prayer.

KENA'ANIM: Canaanites.

KERIAS SHEMA: the prayer proclaiming our belief in one God, recited in daily prayers and at bedtime.

KIDDUSH: the blessing recited over wine on the Sabbath and Festivals.

LAMDAN: a serious student; a scholar.

LASHON HA-RA: evil gossip.

MAZAL TOV: "Congratulations!"

MERAGLIM: spies; scouts.

MEZUZAH: a rolled parchment containing Biblical verses, placed on doorposts in Jewish homes.

MIDDOS: good character traits.

MINCHAH: the afternoon prayer service.

MISHLO'ACH MANOS: portions of food sent to friends on Purim.

MITZVAH (-VOS): Torah commandment(s).

NESHAMAH: the soul.

PARASHAH: the weekly Torah portion.

PASUK (PESUKIM): Torah verse(s).

PASUL: unfit; disqualified for use.

PEYOS: sidelocks.

RABBENU: our teacher.

RASHA: an evil person.

SHANAH TOVAH: "Happy New Year!"

SHEMONEH ESREH: the Eighteen Blessings, or *Amidah* prayer.

SHTREIMEL: (Y.) a fur-trimmed hat worn by chassidim.

SIMCHAH: happiness; a joyous occasion.

SIDDUR: a prayer book.

TALMID CHACHAM: a Torah scholar.

TEHILLIM: Psalms.

TESHUVAH: repentance.

TZADDIK(IM): holy, righteous man (men).

TZEDAKAH: charity; righteousness.

YETZER HA-RA: the evil inclination.

YIRAS SHAMAYIM: fear of God.